Forgive? Forgiven... Yeah Right!
by Linda Lambert Pestana
82 pages, 6x9
ISBN 143712894
PublishAmerica
website: www.twofacesoflove.com

Forgive? Forgiven... Yeah Right!
A Companion Book
by Linda Lambert Pestana
50 pages, 8.5x11
ISBN 0963279300
Annedawn Publishing
website: www.twofacesoflove.com

Two Faces of Love – *a memoir*
by Linda Lambert Pestana
172 pages, 7x10
ISBN 0963279394
Annedawn Publishing
website: www.twofacesoflove.com

Please indicate how you would like Linda to sign your books.
First names are sufficient:

alice

❑ Cash   ❑ Check   ❑ Credit Card

Receipt for total paid to Annedawn Publishing: $ 26.25

First printing

ISBN: 1-4137-1289-4
PUBLISHED BY PUBLISHAMERICA, LLLP
www.publishamerica.com
Baltimore

Printed in the United States of America

Acknowledgements:

Many guiding angels helped me make this book happen—and so I am especially grateful to the following real live angels in my life:

For Josette Fernandes—my friend and editor... for being so intimately involved with this book. I would never have written this book without the many talents and skills and your guiding hand. My thanks could never be big enough.

Don Langevin—thanks for believing in me.

My dear friend and author Gilda Arruda, whose friendship, encouragement, support, and love mean so much to me.

Rev. George Bergin, svd—thank you for your invaluable feedback and for sharing your faith with me.

To William Joaquim III, whose sensitive and artistic talent brought forth the beauty and the spirit of my message—how blessed it is for me to share it on the cover of my book! Thank you!

Special thanks to Brandy Alejandro for her insight, input, and support as the "cover" project was born!

To the memory and living presence of my mother.

To my family—you continue to be an inspiration and a guiding force in my life. I love and honor each of you by name.

To my husband Louis—the forever hero in my life. I love you.

To Jennifer, our dear daughter—you are such a blessing of love in my life.

I am grateful for all those who have walked closely with me throughout my life. Your names are written in my heart.

P.S.: And last but really first—I give forever gratitude to my God.

Dedication:

To my two daughters,

Jennifer Pestana Black
and
Denise Carr Beaudoin

If I ever had the privilege of giving birth...
I would have chosen these two incredible women as my daughters.

Preface

I have a dream, and this is not Martin Luther King speaking—this is Linda Lambert Pestana...

My dream is a dream for everyone. The story within each individual is recognized as a gift. Healing and forgiveness can happen, and that the hurt and scars from the past will indeed remain part of our lives, but—and let me use the word "but"—because we can choose to either allow our lives to become bitter, or we can choose for our lives to become "better" from it.

Now I know that you are perhaps saying—yeah right! But that's my own truth. Let's remember that the past is the past...we cannot relive what we have lived and stop growing. We can keep playing the old reruns, but with that comes anger, resentment—pain—and blame. When we choose to blame someone, we pass our power away, and now we are placing the responsibility for what we feel onto another person.

I could not write these words here if I too had not experienced this journey towards forgiveness within my own heart. It was not an easy experience for me, and I cannot promise that it won't be the same for anyone else. I had to face many long buried memories and difficult, often painful recollections that were probably best left hidden in the past. It was an exhausting and lonely walk through a life filled with many highs and lows, and many times I felt I wore my struggle exposed for the world to see. Much of the memories, experiences and battles I faced, awoke feelings of shame, sorrow and disappointment that I had assumed had healed years before. But I also knew that if I did not remain true to my journey of self-discovery and forgiveness, that these wounds would only scar over and I would never feel fully whole and complete.

My walk through the path to forgiveness did leave me with a special gift, one that I hope will come across within these pages. Both good and bad memories played a tremendous part in my self-healing, and the person I am today reflects the treasure that waited at the end of my inner contemplation. I felt "cured" of much of the unpleasant and unhappy remnants of my past, and through this healing I have developed a greater understanding of what it means to forgive these hurts, those that hurt me, as well as myself.

My wish for you as you walk this journey with me is that you will see the light at the end of your own self-reflection. To heal from past hurts, we must first learn to forgive within. It is only through self-love and self-awareness that we can see past the hurdles in our lives to the blessings that lie beyond. Within all of us lies a beautiful and precious soul, one that need not be burdened with the trials and tribulations of the wrongs in this world. May you see yourself for the essence of pure love that you were created to be.

—Linda Lambert Pestana, July, 2003

Part One-And So It Begins…

Chapter 1

The process of forgiveness is similar to driving a bumper car. Smooth sailing one minute, then SMACK! You hit into an obstacle, back up, and start all over again. Pretty soon the ride ends, but in reality you never really went anywhere except around in circles. So you buy another ticket and ride again.

It's so easy to say "I forgive you," since those are the words we'd rather hear when we've done something we're not too proud of. Many times those words roll easily off the tongue because we've become so accustomed to throwing them around. We've become automatic responders because it's a lot easier to say something and get someone off your back than it is to work out a problem and arrive at a useful conclusion. Why go through all that trouble when you can easily toss out an "I forgive you" and all is right with the world.

In case you didn't notice, the earth just shifted crazily under your feet. Life does not work that way. If it were that easy, I wouldn't feel compelled to share this story with you. But before we get into the "hows" and "whys" of this complex, but healing art called forgiveness, allow me to share a bit of history with you.

To understand who I am, I have to regress to the early years of my life. There was a time when I undertook this process to understand the tolerance and forgiveness of others' shortcomings. I was born in the small industrial town of South Berwick in southern Maine. Families struggled to make ends meet and put food on the table, and mine was no different. There was love and affection in my home, but other, less desirable factors affected my life and the lives of my siblings.

I was the youngest of five children, with an older brother and three older sisters. Our lives were governed by a certain level of instability that was tempered with the only thing that was plentiful in those first years, faith. My father's belief in his dreams repeatedly placed our family at risk. While his goals were lofty, the results were anything but. The glue that held our spirits in check came from my mother.

My mother wasn't capable of recognizing her free will. She was worn out with her inner conflict, and chained to her husband's scale of values. In the process, she was stripped of her identity. But she had her faith, and at the root of it was the small church she often sought for sanctuary, St. Michael's Roman Catholic Church. My father's attempts at "making it" usually met with failure. But in church, there was no failure. Everything clicked within the walls of that hallowed place, and it was there that she could recharge, review, and take comfort that life would get better for her family.

In the span of a few years, we moved several times, mainly because my father was unable to maintain payments on our homes and we would lose them. The worst time came soon after I was born and the family was forced to move to a lonely and desolate place far from the comforts of family and friends. It was during this time away from the relative comfort of our hometown that my mother reached a critical decision. She could face what might come next and sink deeper into a depression that would not leave her, or she would take action.

My parents started out much like any couple in love and embarking on a new life together. They had dreams, plans, and ideas. But my father had other qualities that my mother only learned of as their relationship progressed. He was abusive to her, and his inability to maintain a stable lifestyle for his children was a constant reminder that my mother had little to hold on to. Luckily for her, and for us, faith waited in the wings for moments like these.

In one instance, the home they had worked so hard to build became a symbol of who my father really was. Instead of moving his new family into a home that was built with love, he decided to give it to my grandparents without ever consulting my mother. That day signified a reduction of life for my mother. Yes, her husband had indeed displayed his love for his parents, but in the process he showed her that he had no real love for his new family. He had forced his oppressive and destructive behaviors on her, and this brought my mother an inner despair.

Perhaps the best example I can offer of the torment my father's behaviors caused is the one of my own birth. As my mother lay in the hospital after a trying and life-threatening delivery, she learned the painful truth of my father's infidelity. In the bed next to hers lay the mother of my father's newborn son.

The conflict for my mother was tremendous. At that moment, was it possible for my mother to express her rage and resentment? Would she finally recognize that the life she led was not the one she deserved?

In typical fashion, my mother chose to deal with the situation rather than confront it. Her life lacked inner serenity and companionship. It lacked the reciprocation of marital love, yet she bestowed as much love on her children as she could. The companionship that was so necessary to making a marriage work was not there, and now she had proof that it never would be. But she would not break up her marriage for this. Her concern for what other people would think of her and the stigma a divorce would leave deterred any thoughts of walking away from her abusive and unhealthy life. Regardless of what my father had done, he was still her husband, and they were married for better or worse in the eyes of God and the church. There was no other option as far as she was concerned at the time. She had to make it work.

And how could I describe my father? My father was a self-feeding person. He fed only his own energies and desires, and these were not limited simply to making money. Being a husband didn't alter my father's insatiable drives. He was a slave to immorality. Because of this, my mother always stood in the shadows, wondering when his next edict, strike, or disappearance would come and shake up the fragile family dynamic she worked so hard to maintain.

Such uncertainty took its toll, even on one so strong and resilient as my mother. The move to the isolated seaside town of Wells provided an ultimatum that could not be denied: either the family made a clean break, or it was finished. There was no one to turn to, no church my mother could seek out to pray in and ask for guidance, no food to feed five hungry and growing children. It seemed the family might die out before it even had a chance to flourish.

In the midst of this despair, clarity broke through like the sun after a heavy downpour. Suddenly the answer seemed clear, and my mother knew that the only way to save her children from poverty was to leave. Wells was no place to raise a family. The lack of food, heat, and even the most minimal comforts were a wake up call that we had to get out. And with the faith that had so often guided my mother's footsteps in her own life's journey, Helen Marie Lambert packed up her children and her belongings, and with a renewed sense of courage, returned to South Berwick.

Sadly, faith eventually came with a price. Her beloved church, her respite from the fears she faced in the world, turned its back on her. She was a black spot on the conscience of her congregation. At the time, society had ordained that it was acceptable for a wife to forgive her husband's infidelities. My mother was expected to turn a blind eye to all that my father had put her through. My mother was a unique individual of great courage. In the midst of enveloping darkness and fear, she had often repressed her emotions because she was afraid of the consequences to herself and to her children. This time she would not succumb to the demands of a society that did not honor her spirit. She divorced my father and determined that she could and would have a better life without him.

The church was not so understanding. My mother's bold step into independence was criticized and condemned, and she was excommunicated. Years before she might have acted differently over this declaration from the one place she thought would see her through such a difficult time. My mother would have wanted to shield herself from the world so that it would not know the reality of her circumstances. She would have thought it was a weakness to confess the shame surrounding her life because she would have been afraid of social rejection.

That was not the case. Her true faith was in God, not in the institution that represented him. While the church was her comfort, it was not her sole means of strength. She possessed enough strength of her own to see us through the next phase of our lives. The move back to South Berwick instilled in her that she had the means to succeed where my father had not been able to. The "mortal sin" the church accused her of did not deter her from providing a Catholic education for her children or a roof over their heads that was won through her own hard work. And through all this, she never blamed the church for looking away when she needed it most. She kept on, undeterred by the setback, and all the more determined to prove she could "make it." My mother's mind had unclouded. She had discovered the loneliness in her marriage, and she had refused to remain a slave to her emotional deficiencies.

As far as my father was concerned, he vanished from our lives for a long time. I now realize that my father was guilty of gross inhumanity. He had married and borne children into a life he could not support or provide for. He had many emotions at war within him, but reason was not one of these. I used to wonder what hidden anger did he carry that caused him to strike out at my mother. Where did this rage originate from? Did he gain fulfillment from hearing my mother's distressed cries? Or perhaps he thought punishment would keep her from leaving him? He lacked respect for her, and never put her or the rest of his family first. For that, he lost them all.

Did my father's chords of conscience ever speak to him? In marriage, there is supposed to be love and devotion. He was unable to comprehend this thought, and was also unable to control his impulses and actions. My mother lived a life of inner rage against anyone or anything ever acknowledging these roots to her problems. She wanted release from her emotional bondage, the hold my father's fallibility had on her. In time she achieved it, and one day, he would too.

It took a long time to see that these early experiences did not damage my outlook on life, but in fact shaped it. Our lack of material possessions, money, or a fine home did not diminish the love my family felt for each other. For most people, a house represents a fortress, a place where we can escape and find tranquility from the stresses of everyday life. I had none of this to sustain me in my first years. I was raised in the middle of emotional conflicts, and I grew up tormented with the knowledge of my parents' imperfections.

But that knowledge was not my own. It would take years for me to see that I had not yet come to a place where I could claim my feelings about my family and reach the peace I needed to feel. Salted with the many seasonings of life, I now speak from a place of peace that has allowed me to say "thank you" to all of life. I look back on my first years with a sense of gratitude for my mother's strength, my family's force of will, and my own ability to thrive in the face of uncertainty and hardship. There is no reason to feel ashamed, saddened, or joyless anymore, because I have felt my family's love transcend all of the unhappiness.

I could remain bitter and angry, upset over missed out opportunities or unachieved dreams. But dwelling in my past will not provide a second chance to carry out all of the "what ifs." Any slight I might have thought I endured has eroded away to reveal the strong, assured person I am within. I won't kid you and say the journey to this point was easy. It was intense—I sought, I fought, and I struggled to find meaning in life so that I would be able to cross the bridge to my own heart. I faced many demons, which I call memories, from yesteryear. So hello out there, you are not alone.

Part Two-So What's This Thing Called Forgiveness?

Chapter 2

Do you have enough fingers and toes to count the number of times you have been encouraged to "forgive and forget?" And on several of those occasions, do you recall that you could be persuaded to forgive, but you probably wouldn't be able to forget?

It seems to me that the virtue of forgiveness is highly misunderstood. Our first fallacy is in believing that we always need to ask forgiveness because we have done something wrong. Not true! There are times when we find ourselves outside the circle of comfort that we usually experience with another person. It's not a matter of right or wrong. It's more a matter of being out of step, or not being in sync. Forgiveness can be much like "no fault" insurance. Neither side is to blame; both sides need to share in the repair.

Another fallacy about forgiveness, based upon the belief that I am to be forgiven because I have done something wrong, is that I have to earn forgiveness. We find ourselves asking, "What can I do to make up for the hurt that I have caused you?" Forgiveness is not earned. It is freely given. I may choose to do or say things that will show my eagerness to amend my ways, or show my sincere intention to be the best person I can be. In reality, countless such efforts seldom achieve the desired effect. Forgiveness remains withheld. Why is this? When we forget to free ourselves from the restrictive power that a lack of forgiveness holds over us, we will never achieve the healing we need. And what better place to start than with the most important person we most need to forgive, ourselves?

When I reflect on my earliest impressions, the first phrase that pops into my mind is one I struggled with for a very long time; I was born, but not wanted. No one actually came out and told me that, but it was a palpable presence that haunted me for quite some time. From this one statement, my journey toward the light is where true forgiveness began.

After my mother and father divorced, we were happy for a while on our own. We lived in a stable home, we had food, and we were content. There wasn't a lot of money to go around, but that didn't matter because we had each other.

My mother; however, wasn't happy being by herself. She understood being a wife and mother, and she wanted to experience that feeling again with a man who would love and appreciate her where my father had been unable. My stepfather Bob came into the picture a little while later. In the beginning, he was a good provider and attentive to my mother's needs. Unfortunately, the tranquility we thought was finally permanent would not last.

It almost seemed a miracle. Here was a man who had never been married, and he was willing to take on a ready-made family complete with five kids. My mother thought she was the luckiest woman in the world. And I thought we were lucky too. It became clear rather quickly that Bob was not at all what he seemed to be.

He took us into his home, a small farmhouse out in the country where we had animals, plenty of room to play, and the steady life that growing children need to thrive. But Bob had a hidden drinking problem, and he would vent his frustrations on my mother, as well as my older brother and sisters. My days alternated between child-like bliss and fear that he would come home in one of his states.

My mother tried to make it work. She wanted a good life for us, and despite his faults, Bob gave us more than my father had. We didn't live in a castle, but I believed that no matter where our house was, if we had happy hearts our home was a retreat for love, sharing, laughing, and playing. We children were content for the most part, but not our parents.

We went to St. Michaels Catholic School, and we lived a life that bordered on a fairy tale, at least in the minds of children. But Bob could often shatter that illusion with his destructive behaviors. Despite the fact that my mother bore him two children and kept our home in order, it didn't seem to be enough to shake Bob's addictions and be more of a father and husband to his family. Because of this, I took on the role of protector for my mother. Something deep down warred with the image that I had not been wanted in this family. I had to look out for her no matter what, because I sensed she needed the strength and support my innocence could provide her. I pushed past my apprehensions about my place in the family and rose to her defense like a warrior preparing for battle.

It's quite a picture when you have a five year old clinging desperately to her mother and screaming at the man she has come to know as her father. "Daddy, don't hurt her!" was my battle cry, and in a way I suppose I dared him to take me on instead. My mother had been through so much. Why was this man, my father, doing this to her?

People don't realize the effects that their cruelty and callousness has on an individual. I fought to protect my mother and family, but I also fought to protect myself. It wasn't enough to be strong in the face of danger and disappointment. I had to be a clown too. Comedy for me was the answer to all the disillusionment I felt in my own heart. I wanted to diffuse the tension in my home, and I wanted everyone to be happy. So I became the butt of the joke, the goof, and the klutz whenever I felt it was necessary. And that was a lot.

Clowning around was a shield, a yearning to grow up "normal." Normal, as far as I was concerned, meant there was no unpleasantness in my environment. To a small child, order is the key to feeling any sense of wholeness. I tried to keep order as best I could, but that wasn't always possible. So when the grown-ups were too much for me to handle, I turned my attention elsewhere. As humans we transfer our moods and feelings to wherever we can best relate. Strangely, for me that was animals. Of course, this is a touch and go situation. The goat hated me, the pigs chased me whenever they got the chance, but I think I was okay with the chickens.

But my family was my main focus. I worked so hard to keep my mother safe from my stepfather's tirades, but it wasn't enough. Bob had drifted too far from a healthy sense of reality. His world consisted of alcohol and the disappointments he saw in his family. Our emotions were defenseless. This was an extreme case of violence, and for Bob there was an underlying case of destructive self hate. This inability to reconcile the different parts of his Self was a reflection of Bob's own conflict. And there was nothing any of us could do to help him.

I never let go of my comedy, however. If there was a joke I could tell, a fall I could take, a clumsy move I could pull off for a laugh, I would do it. Part of me needed to take comfort in this aspect of my personality, and part of me still felt ill at ease with my earliest impressions of not being quite welcome in my own family. There was never any evidence of this. I was as loved as my brothers and sisters, but I felt the emptiness as surely as if it had been shouted off a rooftop. Eventually I would come to understand what it all meant.

Because of our need for each other, we were all accepting and approving of one another. My brothers and sisters and I built a special bond, partly as armor against Bob and his disruption in our otherwise steady lives, but mostly because we had all been through so much, and we only had each other to turn to. We conquered our fears together, laughed and played and helped my mother run the farm as well as children could. Everything was a game, perhaps an escape, but it was all done with love. And as a result, we found peace together.

Yet I could not shake my worries that I did not quite fit. My family loved and supported me, both my immediate relatives and those I inherited when my mother married Bob. My aunts, for example, represented the human response to the unjust treatment my stepfather's attitude inflicted on the family. Even though I, like my older siblings, were not Bob's biological children, it did not matter. We were loved just the same by these special people.

Throughout this time, my mother worked her fingers to the bone, but my stepfather didn't seem to notice. He looked the other way, ignored her hard work around the house, or he simply wasn't there. He was conscious of the pain he inflicted on her. He knew it was wrong, yet he never showed any remorse. At least I didn't think so.

The day of reckoning came quickly and painfully. I stood frozen in the other room as I overheard my mother tell a friend that she had not wanted me. My arrival had been unplanned and unwelcome in the poverty-stricken days of my parents' marriage. I suppose some would have run into the room screaming. Others might have withdrawn completely, overwhelmed with the pain such news can bring. But I felt myself change. I realized that I was not enough. I had to be a better child, a good girl, someone my mother would never want to turn away. I would be so perfect that she would never regret my presence in her life.

Most of the time I hid my fear under the cloak of laughter. My comedy routines continued in full force. I was afraid the day might come that I would be shown the door. It took a great deal of soul-searching to finally understand that I would not be thrown out into the cold. My family did love me and want me. But children can be very black and white at times. I didn't comprehend the subtle nuances of love in its many forms. I just knew I had to behave or I would be risking my position in the family.

While I fought to remain close to my family, my mother felt us falling apart. Her marriage to Bob was not working, and she slipped deeper and deeper into a depression that my older siblings were fearful she would not recover from. They took it upon themselves to get my mother out of my stepfather's house. We fled like thieves, basically with only the clothes on our backs. It was a sad end to a life that had initially been filled with such promise. Once again we were on our own with no father to protect us, but this time my mother decided that she would not fall for the wrong man again. Once she divorced Bob and we moved into our own home that she provided for us, she remained devoted to our family for the rest of her life. Once again my mother went through the painful process of liberation, but she was now free to live as she chose. No man would rule over her life again.

Divorce, however, left its mark. People felt we were "different" because we had that stain on our family. They didn't realize what remaining in a violent home would mean for us, but that didn't matter compared to the ugliness of the "D" word. My mother never knew what a balanced married life was like. Divorce was not acceptable in the community or in the church, although she lived a sacrificial life. All of our possessions while we lived with Bob did not add up to the inner peace she felt after the physical and mental abuse ended.

As I explored my feelings on those earlier years and what they meant to me, I was faced with an important question: Why did I feel the need to be perfect to win anyone's love? I knew I was part of a close family unit, despite the trials we'd faced, both with my father and later with Bob. I hid behind the clown paint so well now, fearful that those who might catch a glimpse of the real Linda would turn away from me and realize I wasn't all that special. Deep down inside was a fearful, tearful, scared little Linda, laughing, but really crying on the inside. I coped by blocking my feelings and avoiding the pain. I placed bricks in the dam of my life that held me back from the flow of trust, the flow of love. For me, holding them solidly and as hard as I could kept me safe, or so I thought.

My feelings left me hurt and resentful for a time, but a greater issue obscured them. The problems my family had faced, the difficulties we had overcome—these were not my responsibilities. I was a child, not a superhero. I could no more wish my family into a fairy tale life than I could spin straw into gold. But a child sees life so innocently, and I thought I could do this for them. My first real brush with this thing called forgiveness was the need to look within myself. I had to forgive the young, impressionable Linda. I had to make peace with her fears and dreams for a loving, happy family. She worked so hard to make them want to keep her, when all along they would never have dreamed of giving her away. Instead, I gave away her innocence, and adopted the role of caretaker at far too young an age.

When we choose to forgive those around us, we have to first see past our carefully constructed walls to the vulnerable place within where we hide our secrets. It is only then that healing can begin. If I hadn't started to forgive myself for those earlier, unfounded fears, I would never have been able to reach the next critical event in my life. William Lambert, my father, strolled back into town. With him came confusion, uncertainty, and a sense of unease. What would his presence in my life now mean?

Chapter 3

My father was back in my life. What was I supposed to do?

I was still dealing with my issue of not fitting in. Even though I knew my position in the family was more than safe, I still had my doubts. Would my clown-like appeal wear off? Would my behavior stop being funny and cute, and would I have to go away?

In the midst of this, my father put in an appearance in our lives. Guilt and disappointment had gotten the best of him. He now realized what he had lost when my mother left, even though he had a new family to take care of. But he was determined to be a part of our lives, and to get to know the children he hadn't seen in so long. At first, it was hard relating to a man I had barely known. How could I let my father into my heart when I didn't really know what he even meant to me?

It's hard to know what to do in a situation like this one. The first step is to be aware of a need to improve or increase my phraseology. I grew up being told how important it was to say, "I'm sorry." It has only been in recent years that I have learned that oftentimes that is not enough because the phrase doesn't elicit a response. I can bump into someone at the grocery store and say, "Excuse me" or "I'm sorry" and mean nothing more than a courtesy. I may never see that person again, so why worry?

In other relationships, "I'm sorry" may need to be followed with, "Will you forgive me?" By so doing/saying, I'm asking for a response. The response might be: yes, no, maybe, or "let me think about it." At least I can expect acknowledgment and can anticipate a response. But I must also remember that the gift of forgiveness will not be something that I have earned or that I will pay for at that time or in the future. Forgiveness is freely given!

So what did this mean for my father? He had returned, so to speak, in a prodigal son type of way. Did I let him into my life, or did I hold on to the images I had been given of him. Was I even mature enough to understand the impact of what was going on around me?

In the end, my heart won out. I could not deny how much I wanted a father in my life. And now God had sent him back to my siblings and I. He had admitted his sorrow through tears and grief. With his verbal release came healing. We were able to move past the pain we'd gone through in those earlier years. Life had now reached a stage where we could comfortably be with him and no longer fear for the harmony in our home. He had changed, and in a way, so had we.

Even though he had a different life with a new family, he made time for us in a way he hadn't been able to before. With his realization came his own peace of mind, and we could benefit from that as well. I had been told I was his spitting image. Instead of relying on others' memories of my father, I could now see the similarities for myself.

Sadly, my time with my father was short. He died not long after he returned to our lives. There wasn't enough time to know him, but for the time we did have him back with us, I will be forever grateful. His death closed one chapter in my life and opened another one. I had at last known the love of a father, my real father. We had shared a brief period of togetherness, and I slowly began to realize that I did not have to be the perfect little girl so my parents would love me. My father came back despite my imperfections, and that was what mattered.

This was a very serious thought for a child to ponder. I knew they loved me, but I think I still needed validation. This first area of self-healing could not truly begin until I had made peace with my need to please and feel wanted. I would finally reach such awareness the day my father was buried. Through my mother's tears, she explained to me that had it not been for him, she would not have had me.

It was as if a dam of emotions burst open inside me. My mother had looked past my father's failures. She had forgiven all that he had been. And she had recognized me as a valuable part of her life. It was a precious gift, a miracle I would not have dared to ask for, but one I embraced. I did not need to hide behind my masks. I was included in my family's love for each other. That day changed a lot for me. I began to understand what faith's role was in my mother's life, and what it might be in mine. I also saw that my mother's devotion to God was something I needed to resolve within my own heart.

My father's divorced status kept him from having a traditional Catholic funeral. I knew my father was more than worthy to be in Heaven. He had atoned, and so, if God was as loving and forgiving as everyone said he was, then why shouldn't he find a place for William Lambert too? Whatever or whoever God was to most people, I began to suspect he'd play a much bigger role for me. I wasn't aware of it then, but I would be right.

Life settled into a routine after that. We were finally stable and at peace. There was no longer a father figure around, but that didn't deter us from growing into children my mother would be proud of. Our family unit consisted of my mother, seven children, and my maternal grandmother. We went to school, helped at home, and matured into respectable members of the community. Even the church had accepted my mother once my father died and she was no longer divorced, but now considered widowed. She had her beloved St. Michael's back, and we were content.

The time we had with my father served as a catalyst for the anxiety I felt over "fitting in." My need to be the clown never went away, but it no longer served as an escape for feeling insecure and unwanted. I had healed a part of myself without realizing it. I had learned that Linda could be loved for who she was and the person she would become, and not for what she might be for other people.

This was just one step in a long journey that provided many lessons for healing and learning. I had learned to forgive myself, as well as my father. I had made peace with his imperfections, as well as my own. But the healing wasn't finished. For many of us, the process of forgiveness and healing does not come easily. It needs to be practiced over and over again, and even then our level of success is limited. I had a long way to go before I became truly accepting of the woman I was meant to become. But first I had to tackle puberty.

Chapter 4

We each are born with a spark of life that is uniquely and amazingly our own. We have each shown up in this universe because we have a purpose and a mission to accomplish. We each are born with unique gifts to offer the world, and our mission in life is to discover our gifts and actualize them.

But how do you tell that to a teenage girl?

My teen years were rough, to say the least. I lacked in self-confidence, and was plagued by insecurities. I was afraid of scorn and disapproval. It was a deep-rooted conviction of worthlessness. My self-esteem took a nosedive during those years. My role as the family clown was still there, but it didn't feel right to me anymore. Something was lacking. It was as if a space in my heart was empty, waiting for something to fill it.

I understand my fears now. Back then I had mental anxiety over the need to please people. Instead of being my mother's protector, I felt it was necessary to guarantee her happiness. And if I couldn't do that for her, I blamed myself for failing. I became the "yes" girl. No request was too big or too small. I would do whatever I possibly could for whomever might need me. Throughout my "good deed" phase, I slipped further and further away from the real me. The grasp I'd finally gotten on myself after the death of my father and the understanding that my family did love and need me began to be overshadowed by this dark cloud of oppression. I was no longer living for myself, but for everyone else. It was hard to know who I was anymore, and what I really needed.

My mother began to confide in me, like a best friend would. While I welcomed my mother's trust in my opinion, it was a lot to take on. I had become a support for her, partly from my own doing. I allowed her to reach out to me while I was unsure of what I sought for myself. Not being able to reflect on my own feelings left me drained and heavily burdened. There was only so much I could do, but I always felt I had to do more.

Death touched my family once more while I transitioned from child to adult. I had lost a dear and precious nephew at a very young age. Death and dying was still a touchy subject with me. I understood why someone died after a long and happy life. But why would God decide to take a child?

I wrestled with this thought for quite some time. Where was God's mercy? Did he care about those he left behind? Where did I fit into his picture of things? My insecurities increased. God was supposed to be a loving father. Would he leave me like my father left me? I was empty, drained of emotions. I wanted God in my life. But the bearded, lightening bolt figure of art and history did not sit well with me. I needed a presence I could relate to, one that did not leave me questioning so much. God as a loving father was not for me. But God as a loving mother would do.

I hid my feelings well from the rest of my family. No one knew that behind the bubbly clown lurked an unsure, detached human being. I had them all fooled. But most of all, I had fooled myself. My laughter drowned out the doubts in my head. It was the only way I knew how to cope.

I also shied away from any intimate relationships. I would hang out with friends, go dancing—all the normal activities of an adolescent girl. But dating was not for me. I didn't know why exactly, but it didn't feel right. In retrospect, I lacked the resource of self-love. My mother had gone through so much with two unhappy marriages. I didn't want to end up like that. I thought I'd go to school, become a nurse, and see a little of the world. Yet something else pulled at me, that same, nameless feeling that had followed me for a long while. I was still empty. I didn't yet know what it would take to complete my aching heart.

My need to please people eventually translated into my need to help people. Nursing, however, was not for me. I felt the beginnings of a greater purpose for my life starting to awaken within me. It got to the point where I could no longer ignore what I was feeling. It seemed I was destined to become a nun.

I thought I was crazy. What kind of nun would I make? What if I was using this as an excuse to hide from whatever pain I was feeling? Was this a way to keep from being hurt by anyone in my life? Was I still trying to play the martyr because I felt I had to help everything and everyone? These questions rolled through my mind with the force of a hurricane. I tried to shut them off, but they would push at me, ever more persistent. I had to face my fears, and realize the truth. God wanted me for something else besides wife, mother, or nurse. I would serve, but on her terms.

Even though I inwardly rebelled, other feelings won out. Following a vocation was a hunger that I felt acutely, something that would bring a light into the darkness that I had been struggling against. This was not simple teenage angst. This was a purpose, a decision that I had to be clear about. The rest of my life was at stake. I didn't yet know if I could handle such a level of commitment.

I was afraid to let go of the clown. I wanted to run and hide and forget the notion of being a nun ever entered my head. Who was I to think that I would be cut out for such a life? Me, who had battled with fears of being unloved and unwanted—how was I to express that kind of love and acceptance to everyone I would come in contact with?

I had to heal my insecurities, and heal quickly. I went to visit the Sisters of St. Joseph, the convent in our town where many of the teachers I had in elementary school came from. I needed to reconcile my dual longings. The only way to do this was to face my situation head-on, and pray that clarity would follow.

The sisters were very understanding of my confusion. I spent time at their novitiate in Winslow, a town rather far from my home. I crossed my fingers that this place would feel right, that I would be welcome here. But the ever-present fear that I would not be wanted or accepted snuck in with me, and I found myself at a crossroad. Could I do this? Did I have what it took? Should I run now or wait until the end of my visit and race for the hills?

I did want to run. I wasn't 100% certain, at least not yet. But my heart kept tugging and pulling at my conscience, and I knew that if I didn't try, I would never be sure of what the right decision should have been. I asked to be admitted and was accepted. I then prayed for every obstacle known to man to keep from going back to the novitiate, but God had big plans for me, and nothing was going to stand in the way of this monumental step in my journey. I packed my bags, said good-bye to my family and friends, and went forth.

Regrets and doubts tortured me all the way to Winslow. Was I doing the one thing I feared most? Was I abandoning everyone I loved? I had always worried over whether or not I fit in my family. I panicked that at any time they would turn their backs on me. Was that what I was doing to them? I felt like a hypocrite. I felt like I was finally going home. And I felt ready to crawl into a hole and cry for a week.

I entered the novitiate of the Sisters of St. Joseph spiritually empty, but longing to be filled. There was a lot I had to learn and experience. I didn't know at the time what those things were, but I knew I would find them there.

At least that was the best place to start. The Sisters of St. Joseph would be my new family. They represented what I wanted, even though I wasn't sure what that was yet. My conscience was telling me I needed to be in a serviceable setting. I needed to feel needed, and this was the first place where I could readily face that fact. From then on, I became known as Sister Linda.

I believe that there are no mistakes in life. No matter what happens to us, we can always love and accept ourselves. I am so convinced that we are here on our "earth school" to grow, to open ourselves high and wide, to stretch, and to become! We all have so much to offer, and the cosmos needs you! It needs each of us to be whole and complete.

What this meant for the fledgling Sister Linda, and what it means for each of us, is that despite the fears and apprehensions that follow us throughout our life's journey, we must constantly remind ourselves that we are loved, deserve love, and will constantly receive love. Many times others in our lives will not be aware of these little truths that we've set up for ourselves, and they will not show us the love and concern we need. It is up to us to love ourselves totally and completely. Once we can freely accept that, the rest becomes easier. Others will sense this great love about us and want to share in that. This is how we begin to teach love to spread love. From this also comes forgiveness. Once we see that we are loved no matter what, the hurts we carry are easier to bear, and the hurts others have dealt us can and will be forgiven. I learned it, as have many others. So can you.

Unfortunately, Sister Linda was catching on, but she still had a long way to go.

Part Three-Sister Linda, Heal Thyself

Chapter 5

It was not easy being the new nun on the block. At the time I entered the novitiate, Vatican II was sweeping through traditional Catholic laws and rules like wildfire. I was stuck in the middle of things. There was the old, set way of life for the Catholic nun. On the other hand, the new order that began to prevail in the 1960s changed the perceptions of all religious areas, including the Sisters of St. Joseph.

The good sisters didn't quite know what to do with me. The usual training reserved for the postulancy, the nine month period before first vows, didn't make a lot of sense because I was the only one they had to train. Instead, I was sent off into the community much sooner than I expected. My first job was as an aide at an affiliated nursing home. In a few short weeks, I'd managed to flip the order upside down by my mere presence. I was off into the real world. I didn't know if I was ready, but I was eager to try.

It was a lonely time since I was the only postulate in training. The others were years ahead of me and had already been through the process I was undertaking. My days were filled with study, work, and prayer. I didn't have too much time to consider if my decision had been the right one. For now, it felt comfortable to me, and that's all I really needed to know.

I still had not entirely given up my dream of being a nurse. But I learned quickly that I was not cut out for such a life. Helping people was the easy, enjoyable part of my job. Watching them die was a reminder of the death and disappointment I had experienced in my own life, and the helplessness that came from not being able to do anything about it. I realized I could not continue in this field with the turmoil I felt. And I couldn't ask anyone for help. I had shut myself off so well from needing anyone that I faced my conflicting emotions alone. Again my soul went through the process of grief and pain.

Nursing didn't seem to be the answer, and eventually I was sent to a day care center where I worked with four year olds as a teacher's aide. I also had the chance to live in a convent with other sisters. Here I felt like I fit in. The sisters were all very kind to me, and I seemed to thrive in such an open environment. We ate, prayed, and worked together, and this sense of community appeared to be what I needed to feel secure in my new undertaking.

Not everyone was cut out for such a life, however. One sister with us was very troubled and eventually left the order. Two others departed because the life of a nun was not for them. Throughout these disruptions to our quiet convent life, I felt confused and hurt. I hid my pain behind my work, and pushed away the doubts I felt. But deep inside was the reminder of what I did not want to face: Why did they really leave, and would I want to do the same?

Even though I harbored the occasional doubt about my station in life, I felt God's presence within me. I knew I could draw strength from that, and through my training it became clear that I could rely on this strength to see me through these inner battles. Along with this growing sense of ease within the community, I also felt education was my true calling. I loved working with the children and their families. Here I could be playful, comic Linda, and the context was right for my personality to thrive.

My training had to continue, and I had to return to the novitiate where I would complete my studies and take first vows. I was all alone while I studied and prayed. It felt lonely and empty to be the only one going through the process, even though some of the others declared that I was very lucky to have such an opportunity. I didn't feel all that lucky. I missed people, having friends around, and doing things. Sitting for hours in prayer was uplifting, but a little boring. I wanted to be out in the community with the other sisters.

Of course, while I wanted to share my life and experiences with the others around me, I wasn't so sure about everything else. Some concepts escaped me; such as, the practice that all possessions of the sisters were held as common to all the sisters. We had to share whatever we had, no matter what it was. Ideas of this sort puzzled me, because I felt they went against what we were being trained to do. By enforcing poverty, I didn't feel that this would make any of us free from the constraints of the material world, just unhappy. But I pushed on. I knew I had to fulfill my purpose here at the novitiate.

I was battling a whirlwind of emotions. I fought to maintain the image of bright and happy Sister Linda, but inside I still felt the need to run and never look back. I wasn't unhappy at the novitiate, but I wasn't completely honest with myself either. I had a lot of pent up anger and frustration that I refused

31

to release because it seemed wrong and inappropriate. I had to maintain the image of cheerfulness that everyone had come to expect from me. I couldn't disappoint them, even though I had disappointed myself.

Hiding behind my typical mask, I refused to understand that my fears were grounded in the past, in issues I had not fully resolved before entering the Sisters of St. Joseph. I was barely an adult when I stepped through those doors. How much did I really know of life and what it would take for me to survive in this world? I understood school, friends, my hometown, and my family. The rest was a "learn as you go" experience that left me at times feeling drained and empty. I wasn't sure I was cut out for such a sudden awareness. What pushed me forward was the need to be perfect. That same drive that had forced the young Linda past her fears of a violent stepfather to protect her mother at all costs. Except now I was protecting myself from what the world wanted to throw at me. The shields were up, and I readied for battle.

I finally came to an understanding with both God and myself after many of the sisters I had come to call friends left religious life. To me, it was like experiencing that feeling of abandonment that comes with death. So many of them had been dedicated to the life of a nun, and suddenly they wanted out. I looked deep within to question my own calling. I knew it was time to decide if I was doing the right thing. If I wasn't, now was the time to act. The old rules of the church did not apply anymore. I could say, "No thanks," and be on my way home in no time. But that inner voice, the same one that had nudged me this far, reminded me that this was where I belonged. So I stayed. It felt correct to me, and I wanted to experience life outside the convent walls. I felt my true purpose had not even been reached yet. There were many people out there in need of help, and I wanted to do what I could.

Those early years were quite difficult to get through. I had no real sense in the beginning of what my life would be like as a sister. I wanted to help people. It seemed to be the role I was meant to play in life. From the days where I told jokes to ease my family's pain, I now had a different audience to relate to. But so many insecurities plagued my studies and development. Had I been wrong? Did I make a bad decision?

The answer might be yes and no. In life, we often make the right decision for the wrong reasons, and eventually we find out that we had chosen wisely, that there had been a greater purpose at work all along. My choice to become a nun had been wracked with doubts and insecurities. Part of me felt like I might be running away from myself, from issues I needed to deal with and overcome. I had lost a lot of people in my life, starting with my father. I could have been hiding from additional pain that might come with loss. I could have been in denial over what I really wanted for myself. These are things I may never fully understand. I was so different back then, and so full of questions that I didn't know where to turn. But what I had to do was forgive myself for my doubts. It did not matter anymore how I had come to my decision, but that I had made it. And now I had a new life to look forward to, one I thought I could make a real contribution to.

Forgiveness of self is such a hard concept to understand. While we can readily grasp what it means to forgive someone else, how do you say, "I'm sorry" to your own self? Do you stand in front of a mirror and look contrite and miserable and beg forgiveness of your reflection?

Not quite. Forgiveness waits in our hearts, waiting to be embraced. Forgiveness "hugs" us and longs to be set free. From that, healing happens. I believe, oh yes, I believe that life is more than suffering. It also contains joy, laughter, beauty, peace, and contentment.

So should you stand in that mirror and apologize for past mistakes in your own life? Looking within is the first step to making peace with yourself. Taking a long, hard look leads you on the journey to self-awareness and self-understanding. It was the place I was headed to next.

Chapter 6

I took my first vows in 1971. I was 23, ready to get out into the world, and more than willing to display the traits I'd been trained in. Poverty, simplicity—all this meant I belonged in my community, and I wanted to share that with everyone I came across.

My next assignment was teaching kindergarten. I thought I was ready. I had my plans and ideas all mapped out. I was ready to take on the world. My need for absolute perfection and acceptance was in full force. Bring it on, I thought with an inflated sense of bravado.

The children made mincemeat out of me.

It wasn't that I was a bad teacher. I was an inexperienced teacher. My earlier days at the day care were not sufficient preparation for a traditional classroom setting. I thought a few carefully prepared notes and a kindly disposition would be enough to make it an enjoyable year for the students and me. I was very, very wrong.

The children walked all over me. They instantly picked up on my "newness." I had little control over my classroom for months. Something had to give. Either I would gain some sense of order, or I would most likely go insane. Slowly I got the chaos under control. I developed a sense of which children needed particular kinds of help. Eventually we reached a sort of understanding. I managed to get some learning into them, and in turn, the children began to behave much better.

Both the children and their parents really began to care about their education and the things we were learning in school. I developed a good rapport with many of them, and felt we were at long last making some significant progress. I was now more in tune with my feelings and my calling, and I felt like I was finally making a contribution in the way I wanted.

Of course, it was not all perfect. Life in the small convent had its share of tensions, and the only way I really knew how to deal was through my laughter. I brought out Linda the clown in full force, and at my own expense, I kept us all laughing. Nothing about me was safe from my humor, especially my teeth. I had a pronounced overbite, and used this as a distraction to ease tensions when they ran unbearably high. I was afraid to confront anything I could not handle. Anger and frustration had permeated my early childhood. I did not want to experience more of that in my new home. Because of an urge to please, I would bring attention to myself in order to alleviate someone else's pain. It was a pattern I knew all too well. So, I made them all laugh.

It didn't really matter that I hurt my own feelings in the process of this derogatory behavior. So long as the tension was broken and everyone was happy again, I could make fun of myself. It had always worked in the past. It was sure to work now.

My heart was drowning in pain, but I didn't care. I could rely on my humor to keep our convent life quiet and pulled together. Even when others made fun of me, I let them. I joked right alongside them, thinking how funny it was that we could all be so relaxed with each other. But inside it was a different matter. I was slowly dying, and I did not know how much longer I could keep this up.

I needed the fulfillment of goodness. I needed to feel as if I was making a significant contribution to the community. But I was also taking on too much responsibility for others' woes. One of the sisters became so reliant on my comedy and advice that she was my constant shadow, and I felt terrible saying no to her. But I could not keep denying that I was losing a part of myself. I had spent years overly concerned with everyone else, always making sure they were fine. What about me?

I thought it was selfish to think of me like that. I had to be all things for all people. That was my calling. I could not be focused on myself. It was what we had been taught not to be. But I was in trouble. I had developed an ulcer from all the stress and worry going on in my life. My body finally told me what my head would not admit to. I had to slow down, and I had to think of myself for a change. The superhero mentality had to stop before I made myself worse.

I would like to say that this wake up call was enough to slow me down and get me to think about what I really needed, but it wasn't. I pushed on, determined to contribute even more. I kept teaching, started a degree program at the University of Maine, and I moved to another convent. All the while I kept my feelings repressed and ignored. Sister Linda and the comical Linda were still one and the same. Despite the fact that I was much happier in my new surroundings, I still needed to hide behind my clown persona. If I could make something funny, I would. This hid a lot of "stuff" that I was not yet ready to deal with. Humor was my token of release. The negative feelings whooshed out of me as I laughed, and I persisted in my perfectionist role.

I didn't want anyone to withdraw from the safety net I had wrapped around my life. No one complained too much over my antics, so I kept doing them. I had to feel like I fit in, and this was the only way I knew how. If I had a sense that I belonged here, with the sisters, then I would not question myself too much. I could keep going in the comfortable little world I had created, and not feel too burdened by my insecurities.

By 1976 I had graduated from school and started work on a bachelor's degree. I had also gone back into teaching with a renewed purpose, and began preparations for final vows. It was that last one that left me with a great deal of anxiety. I wasn't sure I was ready. I also didn't know if I was making the right decision. For years I had warred within myself over this, but the moment of truth was coming. Did I have what it took to be a sister? Did I even know what it took to be Linda Lambert?

There was also the added pressure of not knowing whether or not God wanted me. Would the church doors slam closed on my face if I stepped inside unsure of my vows? I knew God loved me and watched over me. But would she also support me if I weren't absolutely certain? Would I have to go it alone?

So much was affecting me that I was wearing out. A close relative was diagnosed with cancer, and a fellow sister took a leave of absence because she was unsure of her calling. Everything was upside down and so confused. It took a while for me to see that I was falling deeper into an exhaustion I could not shake. There wasn't even enough energy to keep up with my comical alter ego. I prayed more often than laughed. It was prayer that centered me and kept everything around me real and able to be handled. When I was focused on my prayers, I was whole and secure. I wasn't really at peace—nothing had so far ever brought me to that point. But I felt connected, a part of all that surrounded me.

I would read the bible, meditate on what I was learning, and pray for all the guidance God could send my way. I still felt like there was something missing in my life. It was the same sort of emptiness I had experienced when I first thought of entering the convent. Now it was back, and I found myself asking a lot of questions. I needed reassurance and comfort. I wanted God to put her arms around me and say, "It's going to be all right. I'll guide you through it." I would pray for hours, hoping for a sign. I didn't think the sky would open up or that I'd pass a burning bush on the street, but I needed some kind of answer.

God didn't disappoint. She filled me with such love and understanding that I didn't feel like I was simply going through the motions anymore. I reached the level of connection I had hoped for. I didn't have to be funny or perfect. I just had to be Linda, and I received my answer.

I had the energy to finish school, start a new job, and physically heal. I also had the courage to face the question of my final vows. I had taken the maximum amount of time, nine years, to reach a decision. I had been so unsure for a long time. While I now felt much more secure in God's love, I also knew I was a long way from fully forgiving my insecurities and fears. I was still fragile, confused, and unsure of how to proceed into the next phase of my life. I was a sister, a teacher, and a member of a loving and caring community. But was this what I truly wanted?

I had to be absolutely sure. This was not a contract I could sign, then later back out of. I was trading one life for a different one. I had issues I had to be certain of, and feelings I had to resolve. I needed to come to peace with obedience, celibacy, and poverty, the hallmarks of entering a vocation. Obedience was not as hard to resolve. I knew that my decisions had to be in keeping with what God wanted for me, not what God wanted from me. I had to be sure that I chose options for the right reasons, not because it was just the way I wanted them. I also knew that many times, my decisions would have to go before a higher authority before they would be approved. Was I willing to live with that? I finally decided that yes, I would accept that aspect of my calling.

Celibacy was another story. I had not experienced the intimacy of a relationship before entering the Sisters of St. Joseph. It was not a question of "What was I missing?" rather than "Will my new life be enough in terms of love and commitment?" Celibacy became harder to grapple with as I got older. Being a wife and mother were things I had thought about, but not given too much attention to. Now the situation was reaching irreversible proportions. I had to be sure that I could translate the love I had in my heart to the members of my community, and not feel as if I had missed out on anything. I wondered if it would have been better to experience love in its varied forms first. As I became more and more in tune with these feelings, I was also very aware of the world outside of my sheltered setting. Inside of me awareness slowly grew. The times were vastly different from when I first entered the convent. Love was a little too free and very available in society to anyone who wanted to take part. That wasn't what I wanted, but I did realize that I could become a wife and mother and not feel that I had done God or the church a disservice.

In the end, I reconciled my feelings with the fact that there were so many in the community that I could give my love to and help without ever feeling as if I had cheated myself out of a traditional opportunity at love. I could give of myself in ways that far surpassed the physical act of love. I could unconditionally love and guide those who needed my help, and feel complete. It would be enough.

Poverty was not about money or possessions, but living a simple life in harmony with what God expected of me. I had to live each day simply and reverently, enjoying and appreciating all of the gifts around me. I had all that I needed, and what I wanted was not about things, but about filling myself with gladness and spirit. I had already come a long way in understanding this. I knew this aspect of my vows would be easy to handle.

The inner rebel wanted to scream in frustration that I was taking this all too well. I had hid my own feelings for so long, afraid of not being perfect or good enough for the church and the community. I didn't want to take orders and have people tell me what I had to do. I also did not want to be tossed out into the cold in case I wasn't completely obedient. I continued on my quest to be the perfect nun without looking back.

I took my final vows and became a Sister of St. Joseph in 1980. I was determined to make this work, and I felt that this was the right decision for me. This was a part of my authentic self, of who I had to become. It was no longer just about me, but about God's plan for me. I had a lot of work to do, and I needed the assurance that I was moving in the right direction. The sisters, the community, God, and my own inner voice assured me that I was.

Chapter 7

The first part of my life consisted of everything that happened to me pre-Sister Linda. Even at the point of my first vows, I was still not fully immersed in the life I had chosen. Now, with the taking of my final vows, I had reached yet another crossroad. Where did my life go from here?

I had been teaching and loving my interactions with the children. But more and more I felt pulled to work with more troubled children outside of a school setting. I thought I might go to school and become a social worker, but first I wanted to be certain. There was no place for me to try out my ideas in Maine. I would have to leave home behind.

I went off to Boston, partly because I needed confirmation that I would be doing the right thing, and partly because I needed to stretch my wings. There were other sisters in Boston who were like me, a little more rebellious, and different enough that I felt I would fit in. I packed my things and left for Boston with a renewed sense that I was headed to a special place in my life.

It didn't start out that way, however. The halfway house where I found a job was not made up of the cute and eager four year olds I was accustomed to. These were older boys, most of them the products of broken homes and abusive lives. They were angry, fearful, and seriously distrusting of adults. And many of them did not take kindly to women.

My first day there was rewarded with a black eye from one of the boys. I represented a scapegoat for their unresolved mother issues, and took the brunt of their pain. During the day I probably would have been better off with a full suit of armor instead of my regular clothes, but I managed. These boys needed stability and guidance in their lives. I hoped I was the one to provide that for them.

At night, no matter how old they were, these boys needed the added reassurance that someone would be there to watch them sleep and make sure the night was kept safe for them. When the sun was out I could barely get close to any of them. But when their heads hit the pillows, each one of them didn't mind being tucked in. The cycle would repeat itself each day, but I was determined that I would see this through. The boys needed love, but they also required a great deal of structure. The older ones were a handful, but I was starting to get through to the younger ones. It was a learning process for all of us.

It did not take too much longer for me to realize that this was not where I belonged. I decided younger children would be more in keeping with my training, and I sought out a new job. But God had other plans. I had been given a new job, lost that one due to funding, and ended up in the one place I did not want to see for a long time, the convent in Winslow. It had now been converted into a Christian Life Center, and they asked me to take over as the Assistant Administrator at the site because the former administrator had died unexpectedly. I wanted to scream no, but my heart wouldn't let me turn down the sisters, so I agreed. I also had to refuse the earlier job I'd taken when the funding came through again because I had committed to the center. With a heavy heart, I packed up and left Boston.

I had just tasted a bit of freedom when it was taken away. I could have said no to the center, but my need to please, and my commitment to my vows kept me from refusing. I didn't know that this was the best choice for me, but I had to see it through. So many key individuals were leaving high posts in our community. Administration and leadership were in chaos, and I wanted to help any way I could. I resolved to try, even though the job was not what I'd initially hoped for.

The job was hard, and very demanding. I was constantly busy in a behind the scenes way, but my heart was not in my work. This was not fulfilling my purpose. I felt out of sorts as I folded towels and sheets and tried to keep my focus on my work. A lot of my job put me in contact with people, so I wasn't completely isolated from my need to interact. But my need to please had once again gotten the better of me. I was unhappy, but I was also not going to overlook my responsibility to my job. My pattern of perfection remained cemented in place.

Not everyone, however, appreciated my attempts. I was told in no uncertain terms that I needed to get over myself, that there was no half-full glass to look at. I was hurt and afraid. Part of me was uncertain what she had meant. I was not trying to sugar coat reality. I was only trying to make everyone happy. At the same time, those feelings of not being good enough to be where I was resurfaced. Was I simply kidding myself? Should I quit while I was ahead and stop trying to be the superhero? I didn't know, but I was sure that

I could no longer offer anything to the situation I was in. I left my position at the center and headed back to teaching. At least there, no one considered my good nature unacceptable.

During that time I was also afforded many opportunities to travel and experience other aspects of the religious life. I went to France, where I not only saw the roots of our order, but also felt the serene joy of Lourdes where the Virgin Mary had appeared so many years ago. Interspersed with these trips was a great deal of prayer and contemplation. I was coming into an awareness of where my life was headed, and my calling really began to make sense to me. I felt renewed, alive, and complete.

I continued to teach, but felt a greater spiritual purpose calling to me. There was a program I wanted to enroll in that would take me to California. There I would study "Creation Spirituality," a new movement in thinking that was more in keeping with the insights I was slowly starting to develop. I was ready to take my request to the community, and eager to start a new chapter in my life.

Sadly, my body did not want to cooperate. I was having serious medical problems, and the doctor finally confirmed what I had dreaded: I would need a hysterectomy. I wanted to fight against his pronouncement, but deep down I knew I had no choice. I was weak and unable to endure further surgeries to avoid having the hysterectomy. I had been a nun for 18 years. The thought of undergoing such a procedure should not have bothered me so much, but the thought that I would no longer be able to create life within me saddened me greatly. It felt as if a part of me had been shut down. The loss was palpable, and my first instinct was to hide from my pain, something I was excellent at doing. But this time I wanted to experience the pain. I wanted to feel grief. I needed an outlet of release, not a withholding of my emotions. I didn't want to be a nun at that moment, just a woman.

I did find peace through the help and healing many in the community offered me. I felt God working through me and reminding me that it was okay to put aside my religious side so I could understand what had happened to me and how I needed to move forward. I was able to come to terms with my loss, and forgive myself and my body for what had happened. I would serve a different purpose in my life. I was not incomplete or less of a woman, but a love-filled being God had special plans for. Thus I was able to physically and spiritually heal.

I had hoped to convince the community to let me attend the program in California. I was still healing, but I was determined to do this for myself, as well as for the benefit I could bring to those I helped. But I first had to deal with yet another tragedy. My oldest brother had passed away.

Bobby Lambert was at a baseball game with his son, and had just scored a hit. As he approached home plate, he collapsed, and died a short time later. He had been suffering with heart trouble for a while, but my family was not prepared for this. I rallied my strength and remained courageous for the rest of my family. I handled details, comforted those who needed it, and suppressed my own feelings. It took a few weeks before it hit me that my brother was really gone.

When I finally understood that he wasn't coming back, the tears burst forth. I cried for everyone, from my father to those who had left the community. I cried for me, for the little girl who had taken on so much and been unable to stay perfect all the time. I cried for the feelings I'd hidden away for so long. Most of all, I cried because I was at last admitting to myself that I could be free from all of my sorrow.

My brother had taught me that I had to take a long, good look at what I wanted for my life. Bobby's life had been filled with difficulty. He had his share of troubles, both personally and with the law. Throughout it all, he tried to find meaning in his life, in his purpose. I finally understood that my brother's funny, laid back personality disguised a much more complex man than I had been allowed to see. He understood that his life was in need of some improvement. He loved his family and wanted to be there for them. But God decided to call him home, and knowing that helped quicken the grieving process for all of us.

We were able to move forward. I persisted in my request to go out to California. Finally, I was granted permission and allowed to attend the next year. I continued in my teaching, and thought life was finally starting to make sense to me. In the midst of all my plans and hopes, I received the one call I had dreaded most. My sister called to tell me my mother had died.

Chapter 8

The thoughts about forgiveness in my life bring about many memories from yesteryear. Many are tightly wrapped in the recesses of my heart, and others lie naked before me; the good, the hard, and the ugly memories.

Early on in my life I witnessed many, what I would call, unfair judgments and criticisms about my family life. When I was a little girl I used to look at people who talked about those who had hurt them and I used to wonder, "Why do people hold on to pain?" I never had an answer. But as I grew up and began to experience my own feelings, I saw the similarities in my own life. Quite simply, hurt hurts. I realized that words go into our bloodstream and travel throughout our spirit.

All kinds of things happen to people; often for no reason. I just lived knowing that terrible things happened in life and it depended on how we chose to survive, how we chose to cope. For me, coping meant holding back from trust and love. I'm not suggesting this was a dynamite expression of action, but I believed that this withholding served a purpose. I was protected from some hurt that I had no other way to deal with at that time. Coming in touch with how to hold back, to pull away, to shut down, to close off, and eventually learning how to open up again were valuable steps to my inner healing and forgiveness.

That meant nothing when my mother died.

I was in shock. I must not have heard my sister correctly. How could my mother be gone? She was everything to me; a parent and friend, someone who had understood me even when I wasn't so sure of myself. I screamed and wailed against the pain that sucked the breath from my body. I heard myself crying out "NO!" over and over again. Somehow the other sisters managed to get me composed and over to my mother's house. I was too numb to be aware of what was happening around me. It felt as if a black hole had swallowed the very essence of my soul. My mother was gone and I couldn't do anything to bring her back.

I stayed in the house for days. Unable to leave my home; the place where we had finally found some measure of stability after those difficult early years. Arrangements were made and carried out, all with mechanical efficiency. It was like acting out a role in a movie. None of it seemed real, but a horrible nightmarish fantasy that would end when the credits rolled.

My mother died quickly, and probably not with a lot of pain. She had been fine one minute, laughing and talking with my sister on the telephone. At some point on the afternoon of November 2, she passed away as she watched television. In an instant, she was gone. The shock was tremendous and left the family cold and empty. What were we to do now?

Greetings and talking with people at my mother's wake was unbearable. The funeral was even worse. A freak storm had prevented a graveside service, and many who had wanted to come were forced to stay home. I had decided to return to the grave site after the weather cleared up a bit to place some flowers there. I was a little too early for the diggers. I watched, frozen, as shovelful after shovelful of dirt echoed off my mother's coffin. Part of me wanted to jump into the hole and stay with my mother forever. Another part of me forced me to stay strong. My brother's death was still a fresh wound in my heart. I didn't believe I had the courage or even the will to face this too, but I knew deep down that I had to. I took a handful of dirt and a white rose and threw them into the grave. This was my only good-bye.

I walked back to the car and sat for a while, wondering what I would do next. There was a lot of love and support around me and my family. I was absolutely certain of that. But there was a lot of pain that we would now have to face. I wasn't sure I was up to the task. I was alone now, with no parents, no one to come home to. It was not the same when I stayed with one of my siblings. I had always counted on my mother's open arms when I visited. Who would hold me now?

We cleaned out her apartment a few days later, more for a sense of closure than out of a pressing need. I stood in the empty place I had called home with my mother's rosary as my only comfort. I studied the spot where she died and said good-bye as best I could. When I felt ready, I walked out and did not look back.

My siblings were very kind to me, extending their homes since I now had no real place to go to. That sense of abandonment crept in on me again. I was without an anchor. I had no foundation to stand on anymore. My life was now my religious community. I had no wise figure to turn to except the sisters and other leaders in the church. I had to rely on myself now, more than ever, to see my destiny through.

I bore guilt too as a result of my mother's passing. She had feared dying alone, and I had promised her she never would. I had never imagined those words would come back to haunt me, but I knew I could never offer that assurance to another human being. I took some solace in the fact that a few days before she died, I had told her over the phone how much I loved her. It would never be enough, but it was all I had left to hold on to.

My mother's death awoke many feelings within me. I had to come to terms with my earlier feelings of not being wanted. I now understood that was not true, but from time to time the doubt haunted me. I had to also understand that death would come no matter what. Everything in this world, from the tiniest plant to the strongest and healthiest human being, had a cycle of life and death to follow. My father, my brother, and my mother had been no different. I had to make peace with that.

I was sad, unsure of who I really was, and disappointed in myself for feeling so lost. But there was one distinct lesson I took from my mother's passing. If we did not experience death, there would be no process of rebirth, growth, and new life. To live, death must be allowed to happen. From there life continues. I wanted to accept such a philosophy. It eased the pain somewhat, because I knew that my family did not die and simply go away. They were still with me, living through my memories and recollections of them. And new life was born every day. God's plan was perfect, flawless. I started to see how this was a learning experience, and this would help me as I embarked on my new journey into "Creation Spirituality." I was ready for the next chapter of my life. My mother had not left me. She would walk the journey with me.

Chapter 9

While I knew I had not completely lost my mother, I still felt the absolute sadness of her death. She was with me in spirit; I still felt her near me. But her physical form was no longer there. I could not walk in my mother's front door anymore and wrap my arms around her. It was a slow, traumatic re-awakening from my grief into the rest of the world. I took my time to regain a sense of myself. When I did start to finally understand where I needed to go next, I knew some of it involved the program out in California. The rest had to come from within me.

I gave myself permission to live, instead of simply existing day to day. I participated in life in ways I never had before. I wasn't fixated on simply pleasing people. Now, I knew I could please myself without feeling guilty. Part of my new awareness was in requesting to be sent to California.

At first, the Provincial Team responsible for saying yes or no to my request wasn't too keen on letting me go. They felt I had been through too much in the past year, and that I might not be spiritually ready for such an undertaking. They also felt that the program, run by a controversial figure named Matthew Fox, might be too radical for the church's peace of mind.

It was a battle of wills, but we reached an agreement. I would attend a few classes closer to home over the summer, classes that were more in line with what I probably should have been taking. In turn, I could attend the program in California, and then report back to Winslow to take over as director of the Christian Life Center. I readily agreed.

The program was exactly what I needed at the time. I met so many people from diverse paths. It did not seem possible that such an eclectic group could grow together in faith and fellowship, but we did. Creation Spirituality brought out life experiences as blessings for growth and awareness. Perhaps my arrival in California was timely. I was able to understand that the losses I had undergone in the past year were steps to my evolvement. I was not the same Sister Linda who had been fairly content teaching four year olds and telling jokes. There was a greater purpose developing inside me, and my new friends and fellow classmates were helping me to see that.

I learned that silence can be a valuable teacher. I also experienced other cultures and ideas in ways I did not realize could be so necessary for growth. We talked, we danced, and we shared our stories with each other as though we were old friends chatting over tea. I described my feelings about myself: how uncomfortable certain parts of my persona made me feel, and how other parts of me felt like true blessings. I told my new family of the pain of losing my ability to bear children. I cried as I related how inadequate my surgery made me feel, and in the process, I reclaimed my life.

I did not think I would be strong enough to see this through. These people were essentially strangers. We would leave the program and most likely never see each other again, and here I was, sharing intimate details of my life. I should have felt exposed, but instead I felt liberated. A deep sense of peace and freedom filled me as comprehension dawned. We were all sharing the same story. Regardless of what had happened to each of us, and no matter what had transpired in our lives, we were all part of the greater good. We were children of the same world, and our individual stories made up the conscience of the universe. There was no shame or denouncement here. We were able to embrace each other as the brothers and sisters we really were.

Perhaps the most important lesson I experienced as a result of the program was the Native American practice of the vision quest. To gain purpose and meaning in our lives, it was necessary to "turn off" the cacophony of daily life and listen to the voice of Spirit that is present in nature. Our journey would consist of a 24-hour period atop a mountain, where we would sit and contemplate in silence over the meaning and direction our lives needed to take. At first I thought I wouldn't be able to make such a commitment. My fears rose to the forefront as I thought of sitting all alone, surrounded by creatures and darkness, all to find out where I was headed next. But a dream clarified my need to make this exception to my fears. I would be okay if I trusted in myself, and in God for always leading me in the right direction. I asked to make the quest, and my instructor agreed. The date scheduled was April 17th, my brother Bobby's birthday. He would have been 50 years old. It was my confirmation that I had made the right decision.

I readied myself for the experience ahead. I fasted and prepared my mind for what was about to take place. On the day of the quest, we met at a sweat lodge for the purification of our minds and spirits. While I had been cleansing my body of toxins, there were still those toxins that were not so easily disposed of. We sat together and prayed to our respective gods. I concentrated my prayers to Jesus, and kept my mother's spirit in my heart.

We were not allowed to take much with us to the places we had each selected for our quests. I had a blanket, my prayer ties that represented each person I wanted to pray for, as well as some photographs of those closest to me. The other few odds and ends I had with me would get me through the night, but this experience was not designed with comfort in mind. We were to remain at our places for the entire 24-hour period, deep in prayer, as others around us, including our assigned sponsors, prayed with us.

By 11:30 in the morning we were ready to start. I said good-bye to my sponsor, removed my shoes before I stepped into my space, and began to pray. I poured my heart into those prayers. I prayed for everyone I knew, didn't know, and may yet come to meet. I was focused and determined, but I also realized I had prayed all I could. I then realized I didn't know what else I should do.

Contemplation seemed like a good idea. I studied the life around me, from the trees and plants to the small creatures in the area. I marveled at the beauty that surrounded me, included me, and interacted with me. It was something I had not necessarily taken for granted in the past, but not something I was expressly aware of. Suddenly I really felt connected to everything around me.

The day passed and I felt a transformation taking place within me. I asked for signs and I received them. I communicated with God on a deeper level than I ever had before and felt her presence within me. I also feared that there might be some unfriendly neighbors in the area of the four-legged, hungry kind, and I prayed for strength and protection. Despite the curiosity of one coyote, nothing harmed me that night.

Unfortunately, the weather was not as concerned with my presence on the mountaintop. It was unusually cold and wet throughout the night, and I was not equipped for the rain. I was freezing, and it was pitch black all around me. I knew I had come to face my darkness, and this was only further confirmation of my lesson in progress. I stood my ground and determined to face my fears as courageously as possible. A little rain wouldn't destroy my spirit. I had worked too hard and lasted too long in this desolate place to lose my nerve now.

At one point I really did think I would give up. I was sure I would not last the night. I felt sick, scared, and ready to call it quits. I had lasted longer than I thought I could, and I had made my point. It was time to go home. But I felt a presence on the mountain with me, and I knew I wasn't alone anymore. Jesus was there with me, as he had been for the entire experience, and my whole life. I felt the strength of his love surround me like the loving arms of a parent, and I knew I would be safe. I would see this through.

I prayed and prayed with gratitude for the blessing of his strength. Morning came soon after and I realized my quest was nearly over. I had not fought my pain, or hid from it, or tried to turn it into something humorous or easier to understand. I had passed through the dark night of the soul unscathed. I dealt with my fears, and there was light at the end of my journey. I had not been consumed by my fears or even tormented by the disappointments of the past. I had a sense of profound peace and awareness; something that had shown itself in bits and pieces throughout my life, but never with this all-encompassing beauty and light. In a way I had freed myself from my demons, and I knew that I had experienced what I had needed to.

When my sponsor came for me, I was ready to tell of my experiences in great detail, but it was not that simple. We were told to remain in a quiet place within, and to refrain from sharing our experiences for a while. We returned to the sweat lodge and the experience was exhilarating. I was tired, hungry, and bursting with insight, yet I basked in the peaceful surroundings and welcomed this final chance to communicate so closely with Spirit.

A week later I shared my story with my teacher. My family had been worried about my well being, but I would not have traded the experience for anything in the world. I had learned so much about myself on that mountaintop. There were parts of me that I would never have discovered in the convent, at home, in school with the children, or even in deep prayer within the sanctity of the church. I had to discover what was at the core of the person I had been, now was, and would become. I think my vision quest offered that to me, and I walked away from it with a sense of peace, tranquility, and fulfillment.

My lessons within the program prepared me for the next phase of my life. I did not yet know that this confrontation with my own darkness would lead me down a path to a life purpose I would never have considered before. I was ready to face the challenges in my life because I felt healed and challenged to push beyond the walls of safety I had always constructed around myself.

Dealing with my grief allowed me to make peace with it. I still mourn my family, but I also know that my time on the mountain helped me to understand where they are now and where I will someday meet them again. I felt them with me then, as I do today. I was able to forgive my insecurities and see my path defined before me. It was not necessary to sit in tearful prayer over the passing of my mother and brother to understand their meanings in my life. It was also very clear that I needed to move forward and not be afraid of what awaited me. And there would be much for me to do once I returned from California.

Part Four-Endings and Beginnings

Chapter 10

I wasn't eager to return to Winslow. I was a different person, and I was not fully conscious of this new me yet. I had to return and immediately take over the responsibility of overseeing the center, as well as filling the shoes of vocation director for the community. It had been such a struggle for me to decide if I had made the right decision when I chose to become a Sister of St. Joseph. Now I had to work with and convince other young women that this might be what God wanted them to do.

It was not easy to keep the center running smoothly. Our purpose in the community was diminishing. We were no longer as valuable a service as we once had been. Rising costs and the increased availability of similar programs in other places made us a bit of a dinosaur. I wanted to make the program work, but my earlier disinterest in the day-to-day workings of such a system began to creep back. I wanted to be out helping people, not stuck behind a desk all day. I needed something worthwhile to do.

I decided to try my hand at hospice work. I wanted to be with people, and I also knew that I had come a long way from the insecure woman who had feared the presence of death in her life. I had always run from it, buried my feelings, and worn a smile when inside I wanted to fall apart. Would I be able to transition into someone who would aid the dying until his or her last breath? I did not know, but I would give myself the opportunity to see if the message I'd received high on that mountaintop in California was the right step in my evolution.

I had avoided dealing with death in any close way for a long time. Coming in contact with individuals who were ready to make that final step in the journey of their lives was both hard and rewarding. I saw so much around me that awoke memories of my own losses, but there was an honor and dignity in being allowed to be present for such an intimate time in someone's life. I was being blessed in a way I did not understand just yet, but I knew I was doing what I needed to do.

From these initial experiences, I decided to become a chaplain in order to work more closely with those readying for the inevitable process of dying. I also knew I could not work at the center much longer because I did not feel I was living up to my potential there, and I needed to train elsewhere; Maine did not have a chaplaincy program that fit my needs. I requested permission to move forward and received it. I went off to Rhode Island to study and embrace the next part of my faith journey.

It was a better time for me in many ways. I was living in a convent with a different order of sisters, but I was able to come and go as I pleased. I attended the chaplaincy program and studied hard as this new aspect of my life unfolded before me. I also had a group of sisters that I met with once a month to discuss where we felt the idea of community was going. We called ourselves "Chaos Community," a bit of a joke on the fact that we really didn't at times know where the community was headed, what we wanted, or where life and faith would next take us. We shared our fears, frustrations, and ideas with each other. In a way it was very liberating to have others of a like-minded vision to talk to and bounce thoughts off of. I didn't feel isolated or alone as our little group met to discuss issues that concerned us as a whole, or to talk over personal conflicts that needed addressing and resolution. I was part of yet another "family," one that accepted me and appreciated my contributions. This was a welcome part of my life, as I learned that my training was not going to be all that simple.

Chaplaincy training was quite involved. Class after class prepared us for the patients we would come in contact with, and our own feelings as we headed out into the world to work with the dying. I was excited about my lessons and was a little daunted by the intensity that some of my instructors displayed. We were pushed hard and criticized when necessary. It was an uncomfortable feeling to have a session with a patient picked apart in front of my classmates, but I also knew I could never enter into this chapter of my life half-heartedly. I would endure what I needed to in order to do the best and most compassionate job I could. I resolved not to let the occasional harshness of the program get to me. God had a greater purpose for me—it was a thought that constantly stayed with me. I would continue forward. I had faced tougher lessons than these in my life already.

Dealing with the patients awakened some feelings in me that I had thought were long since dealt with. I entered into each new situation with the thought that these people had to like me. I wanted to help them, and I would try my best to get them to talk with me and interact a bit. Some of them ignored me.

Others told me to go away and leave them alone. A few would talk and unburden themselves. But I would leave each day wondering how I had failed. What more could I do to get them all to come around?

I was unprepared for the realization that my early, childhood fears of not being wanted were slowly overtaking my feelings about the patients I was in contact with. These strangers were surrogates for me. They reminded me that I had struggled with isolation and disappointment at an early age. I did not want to be so dependent on my childhood feelings, but they came back to haunt me time and time again. I had to push past them. I had not come so far, only to fall back into that negative place.

I tried a new approach. I did not force a confrontation with these people, but quietly announced my presence and my willingness to listen. They were hurt, sick, and most of them had very few people left in the world to care about what happened to them. I would show that I did genuinely care, but I wouldn't make them accept me. Thankfully, my new approach worked.

I interacted with many patients as my training continued. Some were angry at the world, while others felt that God and the church had failed them. I wanted them to know that they were not alone, that God was with them and ready with love and acceptance. Many came away with a sense of peace and completion. No one had ever comforted them in that way before.

My relationships with the patients were also very symbiotic. While they were able to gain something from what I could share with them, I learned a great deal about myself from the lessons they taught me. I found many of my own questions and insecurities reflected in their concerns. My need to be in control all the time, and my perfectionist attitude towards all the undertakings in my life were very apparent in some of the patients I met. These individuals had lives and dreams they might never be able to return to. It was a rude awakening for all of us. At any moment the control we think we have can be snatched away from us, whether by illness or other means. That time became a healing process for me. I changed my process of pruning and shaping my being. I began to cut off the sharp branches of my soul. There was no need to hide within a sturdy cage of self-protection. It was not necessary to be perfect or in control all the time. I realized my lessons had not ended back in California, but were continuing full force.

One of the greatest lessons that came from that time was that it is not always important to know the right thing to say. I was not comfortable with silence, and was usually the first person to speak up or ask a question, anything to break the tension in a room. Even now a little bit of the clown poked through every once in a while. But one patient in particular reminded me that we do not always need noise for comfort. Sometimes a gentle touch and a comforting presence are all that's needed to feel safe, secure, and close to love. The gift of silence is so often overlooked, but had it not been for that patient, I would never have recognized the grace of such a simple act.

Preaching and fancy words were also not always welcome. Another patient taught me that often all that's needed is an understanding ear. Family and friends meant well, but they were unable to grasp the patient's need to simply talk about their illness and deal with its presence. Often we think if we don't discuss something, it's just not there. It was easier to ignore what was happening than to confront it. For many of the patients I came in contact with, the fact that I would just sit and listen to them was a comfort and a release. It was also a gift to be included in their thoughts and fears. I was not family, but I was treated like it. My greatest lessons came from those meetings, and I came away with a renewed sense of myself and of what God wanted me to do.

There was, however, a snag in my training. As I progressed through the program, I did not realize how much anger I carried around inside me. It had built and festered for years under the carefully constructed guise of first, Linda the clown, then Sister Linda. I had never faced this aspect of myself so directly, and I was unprepared for what waited beneath the surface.

There was also one tiny, seemingly unimportant message in the periphery of my conscience that began as a slow nudge, but would manifest itself quite blatantly years later. I was questioning my calling to be a nun.

Chapter 11

Anger was not an emotion I dealt with too directly. I was not supposed to be angry, ever. I was good, perfect little Linda. Whatever upset me or made me unhappy got pushed to the recesses of my conscience. I could not display such a negative emotion when my job was to make everyone else happy.

I didn't want to be forgotten or left behind. I never risked getting angry with anyone because I didn't want them to leave me. So I hid all of my building anger deep down where I thought it was safely hidden away, never to emerge and disrupt the delicate balance I had achieved in my life.

My chaplaincy training brought it all out for me, however. I never realized how much anger I was carrying inside me until I was forced to confront it with my fellow classmates. At that point, my anger knew no bounds.

I was angry with myself for never realizing how much anger I carried around inside me. I was furious with family, friends, as well as aspects of my life I had not questioned in years. I felt the pain once more of my father's abandonment. I was even angry with my mother for leaving me, though I had started to make peace with her passing.

It upset me to know that there were people out there that didn't like me, and that I had trouble getting past this. I angered over acceptance. I couldn't understand why some patients didn't like me or want to talk to me. And I was angry over being criticized about my handling of the patients, my reports, and my classmates' awareness of these things when I could not give voice to them.

I had my writing criticized, which called into question if anyone ever got the points I tried to get across. I felt trapped, useless, and misunderstood. No matter how hard I tried to express my feelings on paper, it was never enough. Was it me? Was I not saying what I needed said? I got defensive and decided the problem was with them. I was more than capable of writing down my feelings. They just couldn't understand me.

I cried, I talked, and I worked my way through this difficult situation. I couldn't believe how much anger I'd saved up over the years. It had eaten away at me and I never really recognized how detrimental this was to my development. My purpose was evolving rapidly, and I was struggling to keep up with it. These issues of anger and disappointment hit at a central issue; I was still struggling with the concept of death.

The finality of death was the ultimate abandonment. It was more than my parents, my brother, or anyone else who had come and gone in my life. I was afraid of their departures. I didn't want to be left alone to fend for myself. I wanted someone to hold my hand and tell me everything was going to be okay. I had resolved a lot of that back in California. But there, it was easier to see past these obstacles. There were no reminders, no tangible clues to the deeper issues I needed to face. Everything was back in Winslow, a million miles away. I could get past my fears on that mountaintop, but they followed me home. I had to deal with them on familiar ground.

Death would continue despite my superhero mentality. I could no more stop it than I could fly. But part of me wanted to put death into a neat little package and put it away where I didn't have to look at it anymore. I knew now that my training was helping me to see past my fears, but that I had to keep moving forward. I could not assume that I had reached a "cure" and that I could continue my work undisturbed by death's presence in my life. I had to make peace with death: its meaning in my life, its place in the cycle of life, and its continued presence in my work. It was the most unlikely of truces, but it was also necessary. I could not be a chaplain if I could not face death.

Finally I completed my training. It was a painful, emotionally trying process. I had confronted my feelings about anger and death, but I had not really applied them in my personal life. My review reminded me that I still had a long way to go. I was not in control. I had to relinquish my vise-like grip on life and let it flow as God intended. I broke down as I realized I was still in denial about death and very angry. I admitted at long last the sadness and struggle of dealing with death. I was not a rock, but a human being. I had a right to feel, and at last I allowed myself permission for that.

I did not suffer in vain. I passed my review that day, and knew I was being called to continue in this direction.

When being asked for forgiveness, the considerations that often come instantly to mind are: Does the person deserve forgiveness because the offense has hurt me, the one who is better (more deserving) than him or her? What will be the advantage to me if I decide to forgive? How will this gesture improve similar situations in the future, by guaranteeing that the same offense will not be repeated?

Trying to put these thoughts aside, I see the focus to be upon such concerns as: Does the infraction merit forgiveness? Does withholding forgiveness accomplish anything positive? Can I realize the joy of offering forgiveness and see the relief on the face of the person asking?

Among my biggest struggles is offering forgiveness to someone who has not asked for it. Most often the other person doesn't have a clue why I am so cold or harsh towards him or her. Until mind reading becomes popular again, my choices are: 1) Find a way to discuss my feelings of anger with the person, or 2) Let it go! Now there's a phrase that we're beginning to hear more often. But the question is, how?

Some of the same concerns over this issue are much like the previous ones we've covered. Is it worth the personal aggravation to hold on to past hurts? Does the different level of status (I'm better) between us mean that much? How can I be sure the hurt was intentional? Would I like to credit myself as a giver of the gift of forgiveness? As you can imagine, the greater the time lapse, the greater the rift, and the greater the danger of not being able to make amends.

All I had to do was apply this to myself.

Chapter 12

I had come a long way, but there was still much I needed to learn. I had faced my fears and overcome them. I had also confronted death and my anger over it and succeeded there too. But I was still in denial about my need to feel needed. No matter what had happened to me up until this next phase in my life, the issue of not being wanted still plagued me.

I had a new job waiting for me once I completed my program. St. Anne's Hospital in Fall River, Massachusetts needed a chaplain, and this would be my new role. I also decided that the time had come for me to try living on my own. I had so much on my plate that I needed the quiet and freedom living alone would afford me. Permission was granted, and I moved into my new home and job with high hopes that I would be making a difference. I was also selected as a delegate to represent the community at the international General Chapter in France. At first I was not a guaranteed choice. I waited through three torturous elections before my name was selected. Some felt I was not the best person to go. I could sense the old familiar stirrings of not fitting in, within me. I was upset and angry that I was still experiencing this, and that the community did not have faith in me that I could represent them appropriately. All of this led to a feeling of increased disillusionment with Winslow and my place there. But I was happy with other parts of my life, so I pushed on.

I worked with a team of religious professionals that were as dedicated as I felt I was to helping and caring for the terminally ill. We offered support, patience, kindness and a ready ear to all of the patients who needed someone to turn to. It was a rewarding and fulfilling experience. I was able to apply all of my training and really make a difference in the lives of these patients. They in turn taught me even more about myself and where I was headed in my new undertaking.

Many of these patients felt cheated, incomplete, and unable to communicate with their families and friends about what they were feeling.

We provided that chance for release, and a way for them to feel human again, not just patients or numbers on a chart. The doctors and nurses were extremely busy and had many of their own issues to deal with. We were able to work around the medical aspect of patient care and treatment and see the patients for the people they wanted to be recognized for.

Some of the patients healed. Treatments were administered and were successful, and they were able to go home and resume life once again. Other patients were not so lucky. Some of them knew their time was short, and they simply wanted a hand to hold or a few words of comfort as they made peace with the coming difficulties ahead. Often I would just sit and be with a patient because a calming presence was reassurance enough that they were not abandoned in this life. While they took comfort from this, I was able to draw a little strength as well. But there were other issues, bigger ones that I would yet have to face.

I went to France, and while the trip itself was enjoyable, the work we did was much less so. There were rifts within the relationships between the delegates. No one wanted to compromise or even agree to disagree. It seemed we were to butt heads for the two weeks we would remain in France. The other delegations were getting along just fine, but the one from Winslow was not faring too well.

I was feeling empty and disappointed at our inability to get along. I asked for guidance and hoped we would make it through the next two weeks without too much difficulty. I was increasingly distracted by the tension in our meetings, and was unable to focus on the true purpose we were sent their to achieve. When we returned home, I decided that despite the troubles we'd faced in France, I would renew my resolve to work towards a better understanding of my faith and where it was taking me. I returned to work with purpose and a hope that I was moving forward and gaining spiritual ground.

Each patient I came across had to undertake such a traumatic journey forward. Many of them looked at their impending deaths with a sense of guilt and failure. Lives were not properly lived, decisions were poorly made— all of these weighed heavily on many of the people I met. Some of them did not think they were worthy of forgiveness, while others felt that they had lived in vain and there was only sorrow awaiting them at journey's end. Many of them also felt very alone, as if they had to suffer silently and without any comfort. No one else could understand what these people were going through; the path was a solitary one.

I offered care as best I could. Some asked for the Eucharist, while others wondered if God would accept them into Heaven when they died. I provided all the strength, love, and encouragement they needed, as well as what I could freely give. I had experienced the other side of death. I had been the grieving daughter, sister, and friend. I would console them and bring what measure of peace I could.

It was not only a question of helping the dying, but those they left behind as well. Many of the family and friends were upset, angry, and empty over the impending loss of their loved ones. I related well with this aspect of pastoral care. I had seen what they had seen, and experienced the many emotions that came with learning someone we loved was about to die. In my case, those I had loved were taken suddenly and I had no warning that they were about to leave. There was some small comfort in knowing that these people, for the most part, would have the chance to say good-bye.

It was not important to clarify the "hows" and "whys" of dying; it was important simply to be there. I was needed for a hug, a kind word, or a reassuring smile, and not for the years of training I had undergone. While this was necessary so that I could offer all the help needed to those I came in contact with, it paled next to the need for a friend or a shoulder to cry on. Many of them needed to blame someone or something for their loss. God was a popular figure in these cases. They could not understand how such a loving figure could be so cruel to take away their mother, son, or friend. It would take some understanding on both our parts. I told them that I did not know why it had to be this way, but that I could be there with them. Together, we were all able to find a measure of peace in the reassuring presence of the other.

I felt fulfilled and useful in the work I was doing. This was where I belonged. But an increasing sense of emptiness plagued me, a feeling that was harder and harder to ignore. I could not deny that something was missing, but I was afraid to put too much thought into it. I wasn't sure what I would find, but it was becoming apparent that I had to confront this issue soon. I was offering the patients I worked with all the time and chances they needed to express their fears and feelings, but I was closing myself off from the same opportunities. I couldn't do this to myself anymore. It had been my pattern for so long. Its familiarity made it an almost detested part of me, and I longed to simply give voice to whatever was at war within me.

The expression of "LOVE" is lived out with each waking moment, awed with its many different faces. I had seen that love time and again as I talked to and comforted the patients in my care. The responsibility to love and the responsibility to forgive rest in our own hearts. As I reflected upon life's many unfolding changes within my own life, I realized that each event lifted my awareness of life, forgiveness, and healing to a deeper and more reflective place of peace. It would be this knowledge that would guide me to the next phase in my journey of faith. I had done much work to heal myself, forgive my fears, and find self-love. Now I had to question my true purpose.

Chapter 13

My life now had a sense of order. I worked at a job I loved, had my own apartment, and yet I still remained very close to my community. It was during this period of growth and awareness that I met Debbie Pestana.

We first met in 1993. That meeting didn't seem monumental, at first. I had entered her room and introduced myself, and offered Debbie Communion. She had accepted and I said good night. My trip to France kept me from seeing her or any of my other patients for two weeks.

When I returned, I learned Debbie was eager to see me again. I visited with her when I could, and we became friends. She was different, more animated and content when we talked, at least that was what her husband confided to me. I wanted to help her as much as I could. If I could aid Debbie in maintaining a positive mental outlook for both her and her family, then I would do what was necessary. This included house calls when Debbie was feeling especially down, and long afternoon talks to bolster her spirits and keep her focused on her recovery.

Debbie did not discuss death, as was the case with some of the patients I worked with. For her, dying was an avoided issue, and one that her family did not address either. I learned early on in my pastoral training that I had to be at the same place as the patient. In time, if she felt comfortable, she might talk to me of these things. For now, I would be her friend and caregiver, and offer all the love and acceptance she needed.

In the meantime, I was nominated for the position of Formation Director in the community. With this potential position came tremendous responsibility. The attraction to religious life was not exactly overwhelming, and I knew that the existing program would have to undergo a major revision for it to be successful. I was in conversation with another sister over the potential for this new program, as well as the nuts and bolts of Formation itself.

Part of me thought this might be a new opportunity to bring the community into a more modern environment. The chance to move the community's focus from Maine to Massachusetts would also be a challenge. But the voice of acquiescence and the voice of rebellion debated within me. For all of my religious life, I had always done what was asked of me. I had never refused an assignment or a request, even when it did not feel correct to me or I was not happy to undertake a new role. But something was different inside me. I was not so willing to simply go along with what the community wanted me to do. I was ready to branch out into areas that I wanted to explore, and not because I was told I had to.

I was also immersed in my chaplaincy at St. Anne's. While I saw many patients on a daily basis, I only saw Debbie Pestana a few times when she was in the hospital for treatments. Debbie and her family were often taking trips together in between her treatments. Her husband Louie wanted to make sure she was happy and had things to look forward to. It was their way of dealing with the inevitability of her illness, and it brought them all closer. And Debbie would always remember to bring me a little souvenir from each of these excursions.

When we would talk, I did most of the talking. Debbie listened to me and understood what the process of dying would mean in her life, but she was not yet ready to give voice to such thoughts. Her cancer was an ever-present reminder of the short time she had on earth. She wanted to pray with me and discuss common, everyday things, and limit the focus on death. I got through what I could, and continued to be her friend throughout her difficult time. I hoped what I did manage to share might help her and make some sort of impact, and I prayed that would be enough for now.

By now it seemed that my world was entering a chaotic phase. Formation was still a sensitive topic, and while many felt I could offer the position the strength it needed, my little community, "Chaos Community," felt that I would not be able to offer them the attention we had strived for all this time. I wanted to be there for them, but I also knew that I had much I needed to do on my own. Chaos Community was a division from the community, and that was the very issue I was trying to avoid with my ideas for Formation. I couldn't be all things to all people anymore, and when Chaos Community had first come together, I was in a place of uncertainty. I wanted them to support my hopes and wishes for a new approach to the community, but many of them felt I was fighting a lost cause. I would not achieve anything by trying to change the system, they insisted. I would simply get caught in it.

I felt differently. I wasn't sure what type of difference I would make, but

I knew I had to try. I continued to come up with ideas with the other nominee for Formation. Unfortunately, it was becoming increasingly apparent that I would not make much headway there either. We were unable to agree on simple administrative ideas. I felt as though there was no support at all available to me. In some ways, I wanted the decision on Formation made once and for all. At least I would know where to go next.

I was feeling lost again. I wanted to help, but I also felt like no one wanted to make an effort to see this project through. I was caught between my desire to do what was right and the increasing disquiet in my heart. Something wasn't right, and I could not put my finger on it. During this time, I also learned that Debbie Pestana's cancer was spreading, and that death was much closer than the family had expected. While her condition did level out somewhat afterwards, her situation was not good, and while my anxiety over formation reached frantic proportions, Debbie took a turn for the worse.

Debbie's health was failing rapidly. It was late August, and she felt the end approaching. She asked me to look after her family when she died. Her husband Louie and her daughter Jennifer would need someone there with them. I agreed to do what I could. I felt that strange nudge in my heart that had always exposed my emptiness and disappointment. This time, however, it was trying to tell me something else. At the time, I had no idea what that might be.

Debbie Pestana died at home on September 10th, surrounded by family and friends. She had expressed her desire to live, but the cancer was beyond any medicine at that point. She feared that no one would be there to watch over her family. It was a telling thought that would have important repercussions later on.

I considered Debbie a friend, and I was closer to her than most of the patients I worked with. Our connection was strong, and I learned that she had passed away not long after I had called to see how she was. I immediately went to the family home to help in any way I could. I prepared a prayer service for her, and attended the funeral services. In the short time I'd known her, I considered Debbie a friend, as well as a courageous example of life. She had wanted so much to keep going, for herself and for her loved ones. She brought an important and necessary lesson into my own life as well. I felt the safety of my comfortable world starting to slip from me, and deep down I sensed it would only be a matter of time before everything fell apart.

Chapter 14

It felt as though I were on a collision course with reality. Formation was put on hold. It finally occurred to me that no one really wanted the job anyway, and what had seemed like a fresh opportunity was in truth just another assignment that would again take me away from the essence of my faith journey.

I could not see eye to eye with the other sister working with me. She was unwilling to commit to a simple living arrangement, so the issue of working together as co-directors was pretty moot. We were unable to focus on what was needed to get Formation into a workable situation, and the committee decided it would be best to wait.

I also had no support from anyone. Chaos Community had been my rock, but we were also at a crossroads with each other. I could not keep going without some sense of order, nor could I ignore the emotions at war within me any longer.

I felt like the victim in all this upheaval, even though I didn't want to see myself that way. I was breaking up inside, and I had no sense of where I was headed, or even if I knew what I wanted to do. For 25 years, I had done my best to fit into whatever situation came my way. I had been afraid of diverting from what others wanted of me. The agonizing truth was that I recognized the resistance and the need to fit in. I also realized that everyone had to face their own shortcomings. I had done my best to be what I could for every situation and obstacle that came my way. I also realized that I didn't want to be a nun anymore.

At first I was shocked. I had never given voice to such feelings, yet they had been there for quite some time, waiting just below my radar. I was pushing myself too hard, and I wanted to be more than was needed of me. I wasn't that superhero that I'd wrestled with for years. I wanted to try life on my own terms, but I didn't know what to do next. Life outside the community was an alien world. What would I do? How could I fit in? Was there a place for me in secular life? I had thought there was one in religious life. What if I was wrong again? What would come after that?

During this period of uncertainty, I continued with my routine. I worked, and ran a bi-weekly cancer support group I had started quite some time ago, "Footsteps." Debbie's husband Louie had been an occasional visitor to the group, and through his work with us, he was able to gather the courage he needed to visit Debbie's grave. He asked me to go with him, and I agreed. I had promised Debbie I would help her family if I could, but I had not been prepared for what would happen next.

I reached out to comfort Louie as we stood together by Debbie's grave, and something inside me shifted. I looked at Louie, but did not see a man simply in need of comfort. Other, more unfamiliar feelings stirred within me. I was experiencing a new awareness, that of a woman over a man she cares for. My instincts rebelled. What was wrong with me? I wasn't ready to deal with any of this. I couldn't have these feelings for a man. I was a nun, and a dedicated one, despite my recent uncertainties. I had never been interested in a relationship with anyone, and here I was, feeling things for a man who had recently lost his wife and was still grieving. I wanted nothing to do with the emotions commanding attention inside me. I wanted to retreat into the safety of life as I knew it and forget about what had transpired in the cemetery. I also wanted to wipe the slate clean. When I did decide to put religious life behind me and venture out into secular life, I wanted to get far from home and start new.

I was still experiencing a profound emptiness and loneliness that would not leave me. Counseling seemed like a good idea, but before I approached the possibility, I did some internal exploration of my own. I was weary of religious life. I had struggled for 25 years to find myself within the structure of the community, and in many ways, I had. But I was also unable to shake the sense that there was something more out there for me, that God was calling me to a new place in my life. I owed it to myself to explore this new possibility. I just didn't know what it would involve.

I also had to deal with these feelings I had for Louie. I had no idea if he might feel anything at all for me. I had kept everything inside, as was my usual fashion. I did not know if there was any chance there for something to develop, and I was afraid to even consider it. My life was scattered in bits and pieces around me. I did not know where to turn to next.

Work was my only saving grace. I functioned while inside the hospital's walls, but I could not keep it together once I walked in the door of my apartment. The weight of my confusion was crushing me, and I had no outlet, no means to understand what was happening inside my head or my heart.

I sought out a psychologist on the advice of my spiritual director. I couldn't keep hiding behind the "Linda the clown" persona. I was tired of smiling in the face of my pain. I needed to gain some clarity, and I also wanted some answers. I thought therapy might help me. The psychologist offered me a bit of soul work. He told me to go inside myself and see what I would find there. I had to look deeply within my heart and find what I needed to look at. It would be difficult, he warned, but necessary. I was willing to try anything.

My discovery was profound; fear had kept me locked in a battle of wills for years. I fought my rebellious nature and at the same time I tried to maintain a level of perfection that was inconceivable. I stared long and hard at the dark corners of my heart and found years of built up anxiety and fear lurking there. I was unable to break free from the cycle because of my need to please everyone and be a model daughter, sister, nun, chaplain, and friend. I was pushing beyond the human limits of endurance, and digging myself deeper into a melancholy that was becoming harder to shake.

I had to also face the fact that I was harboring a few inherited fears. My mother's fear of other people's disappointments and expectations had carved out a place in my soul. I had carried that with me all this time, and it had eaten away at my ability to believe in myself and what I was capable of. I had spent too long living up to what everyone else wanted. I had forgotten all about my own needs.

I had the ability to choose. I always had, but I placed so much fear between myself and choice that I had lost sight of that option in my life. I feared leaving religious life. I did not know what would become of me once I made the conscious decision to move on. But I was also afraid of how I would feel if I stayed. It was wrong to remain in a situation where I could no longer grow. But I did not want to lose that safety net. Instead, I paralyzed my life and simply existed.

I wanted to take the next step, but I did not know how, or if I even had enough courage to try. I contacted my Provincial and poured my heart out to her. I shared my anxieties, my fears, my reasons for seeking a new life, and my need for understanding and compassion. She felt my struggle, and together we cried over the next phase in my journey. My mind was now made up. I would leave religious life.

I had sealed myself behind a wall of fear for a very long time. I hid my early fears of being unwanted behind a mask of humor and comedy. I thought I could win my way into the hearts of my family. Even though I learned early on that they did love me unconditionally, I was unable to shake that feeling loose. For many years it would follow me like a dark, cold shadow. I was trapped within my own creation.

When I got older, my clown persona shared center stage with perfect Linda. I was the best daughter, sister, and nun. I was everything anyone could want in a relative or friend. And I was slowly losing pieces of myself. I couldn't keep up the pretense of being 100% all the time, but I pushed on until I was ready to collapse from the self-imposed weight of responsibility this carried. I was bereft of strength and energy. I just couldn't give anymore.

A lot of my time was spent crying in those first days of awareness and acceptance. I could not share my feelings freely; many would not understand my reasons for leaving. I told the sisters in Chaos Community, but they were insistent that I stay. I knew then that this was one journey I would have to undertake alone. I left St. Anne's with a simple explanation of the need to move back to Maine. Few people knew my real reason. I could not explain that I had come to a turning point in my life and that I needed to focus and proceed into this new venture with a pure heart and a full understanding of what God now wanted me to do. I simply said good-bye, accepted their best wishes, and left.

I was unsure how many would take my news. I knew that people would form their own opinions over what happened to make me leave, so I kept my decision fairly secret. I signed the papers for my official dispensation 25 years to the day of my entrance into the community of the Sisters of St. Joseph. I signed my name with a clear and direct purpose of what I had to do for my growth and evolvement. I had served God as best I could in this one phase of my life, but now I was being called to serve in a different way. And apparently, God did not want me to enter into this next phase alone. I would now have another person to share the journey with, Louie.

Part Five-A New Chapter

Chapter 15

I did not know if I would have the strength for the next phase of my life.
It was painfully difficult to give up religious life. I had known the life of a
nun for 25 years. What would the next step in my journey be now?

I lived in a daze for the first few weeks. I wasn't sure where I was headed,
but one thing was clear; I was starting a new chapter in my life, and I had to
be ready. I packed up my things and prepared to leave Fall River. My body
had started telling me that I needed to slow down and take better care of
myself. I was in a lot of pain, but I was also eager to move forward. I had a
future to consider, and I had to decide who might play a part in it.

A short time before my dispensation became final, Louie had invited me
to dinner with his daughter and in-laws. Up until then we had been good
friends, and the strange, unfamiliar feelings I had experienced that day in the
cemetery were stashed away in the back of my mind. I had said I would look
after these people, and I wanted to keep my word. Dinner, however, turned
out to be a two person excursion. Louie and I were the only ones able to
make it, and we spent a great deal of the evening talking and sharing stories.
I unburdened my heart as I described my uncertainties over religious life,
and my decision to leave. Louie listened, and he understood. I felt a weight
lift as I realized here was a friend I could relate to and who accepted my
decision for what it was.

But Louie did have one surprise for me. Louie looked at me and asked if
I had left the community for him. I was momentarily speechless. I quickly
replied that no, it had nothing to do with him, but I began to wonder. Was he
feeling for me any of what I was feeling for him? The thought brought a light
flutter to my stomach. Louie's question certainly sounded like it might be
the first recognition of romantic feelings for me, but I wasn't sure. Was this
the beginning of something good between us?   At that very moment, I
dared not visualize the dream. I understood little of it, yet I knew the seed

had been planted.

At the time, however, it was difficult to express these growing feelings. I was still part of the community, even though the papers were nearly finalized and it would only be a short time before I received my dispensation. Louie and I were careful not to be seen together. We could not announce to anyone that we were seeing each other. It would be assumed that perhaps I did leave the community for Louie, and that was the sort of sensationalism that I wanted to avoid. I did not want to cheapen our relationship by hiding it, but I also did not want it to be tainted by others' misperceptions and interpretations. What I shared with Louie was special and filled with respect and appreciation, and I wanted it to stay that way.

We were also undergoing our own expressions of grief. Debbie was still a strong part of Louie's life, and he had not completed his grieving for her. I was grieving my departure from the community and my life as a Sister of St. Joseph. It had been an indispensable part of my nature for so long, and it did feel as if part of me had died. What I did not yet know was that a new Linda was waiting to be born.

After I left Fall River, I spent some time with my sister's family in New Hampshire. It was a debriefing of sorts. I was able to regroup and explore my experiences of the past few months in a neutral setting. I had left the community on good terms, but I now had to face the fact that I was not a nun anymore. I was an average woman trying to make it through life, just like everyone else. The thought was monumental. I wasn't sure I was ready. I knew I had made the right choice, but there was so much out there that I had never experienced, and a lot I didn't even know existed. I had some time to make up for, all while getting my emotions in order and deciding where Louie fit into all of this.

I had been a caretaker for others for so long, but I never thought to look inside of my own self. I had no instructions on how to love myself. It seemed almost selfish to consider my new life when I had never allowed myself to feel that way before. Through all of these warring emotions, Louie was there to help me.

I had seen Louie's devotion to Debbie, and had experienced his pain and sorrow with him at the time of her passing. He had a tremendous respect for her presence in his life, and I marveled at how different he was from the other male figures that had influenced my life, especially while I was growing up. His humor, sense of self, and the way he kept his family safe were all commendable qualities that I found appealing in his personality. And as time passed, I found I was falling in love with him.

Our friendship was progressing in a comfortable, easy manner. Louie and I had seen each other through some very painful and devastating experiences. I had shed quite a few tears in front of him, as he had in front of me. We were not embarrassed to express our feelings in each other's presence. I felt appreciated, understood, and at peace with him. But Louie was struggling. He still mourned for Debbie, but he had feelings for me, and this caused him a great deal of confusion.

We did, however, love each other, and we were both determined to see where this new path God had set us on would lead us. Life has many unforeseen circumstances, and there is a mystery to it all, so much so that I would find myself lost for words to explain how our love developed. At times I would tremble with the knowing that I felt totally secure with my love for Louie. I also knew that he felt the same way.

There were other people that we had to consider as we embarked on this relationship. Debbie's parents, Mary and Sid, did not know me as anyone but Sister Linda, and now I was dating their son-in-law. It would take a great deal of understanding from all of us as we transitioned past such a distinct label to a more connected relationship with them.

Louie and Debbie's daughter Jennifer was my greatest concern. I was fearful that she would consider me a replacement of her mother. I wanted to reassure her that I was there for her as Linda, not as a stand-in for anyone else. But I also didn't expect a Brady Bunch moment of hugs and kisses when I spoke to her about my relationship with Louie. I prayed for guidance and a way to express my feelings in a genuine and kind way.

My relationship with Louie would bring change, but I wanted Jennifer to know that her father's love for her mother would never falter and still lived within him. I would not be a substitute for Debbie. I knew I had to open my heart to the experience, and when I did finally speak with Jennifer, we reached an understanding. She accepted my presence, though she said she needed some time for the adjustment. Deep down I knew I would never be able to hurt this child, and I said that I would walk away from my relationship with her father. I did not want to cause a rift between father and daughter. I was stepping into a ready-made family, and I would not be the cause of its break-up.

Thankfully, I did not have to walk away. Louie and I continued our relationship, and I saw him every weekend. We dated regularly, and his family was genuinely happy for us, as was mine. Our relationship felt right and blessed, and I pushed forward, determined to see this work. We did have our share of troubles though. News of our relationship was not welcome to some of Louie's friends, nor was it respected within the halls of St. Anne's. We faced scrutiny and rumor as we spent time together and got to know each other. I knew we weren't doing anything wrong, despite the lies being told about us. We supported each other in those days, unwilling to let anyone spoil the healthy, caring relationship we had.

Unfortunately, my body was not cooperating very well anymore. I drove down from New Hampshire each weekend to see him and Jennifer in Swansea, Massachusetts, and the commute was taking its toll. My back was a mess, as well as the rest of me. I wasn't able to drive such long distances as well as I once had. Louie then surprised me once more. He asked me to stay in his home with him and his daughter.

While I visited him on the weekends, I stayed at Louie's home. It had always been a respectable arrangement, and it would continue to be so until we got married. We decided on October as an appropriate month to be married. Things were moving very rapidly, but despite the speed of our relationship, we agreed that a year would be an appropriate time to wait before we made our commitment official. Debbie had passed away not too long ago, and we wanted to respect her parent's feelings, and most of all, Jennifer's. I wanted to make sure everyone was comfortable with the arrangements, and that feelings would not be offended.

Moving in was a tremendous adjustment for everyone. I walked into a ready-made family, but they also had a life I needed to adapt to. Debbie's personal signature was everywhere I looked. It was hard not to feel like an outsider in a place I was to now consider as my home too. Slowly I started to adapt, and I prayed that it would feel like my home, one day soon.

Although I wanted to maintain my independence, my attention was focused on Jennifer. Fears can make you do two things: they can harden you and make you unwell, or they can make you confront them and move past the fears to the lessons beyond. Jennifer was going through an emotional roller coaster, and I didn't want my fears to affect her. I wanted to confront my fears of this new life, but I also wanted to maintain a comfortable space between us. I wanted Jennifer to feel she had a friend in me. She was experiencing detachment from her mother, and attachment to a woman whose presence essentially amounted to taking her mother's place.

At first, Jennifer had a hard time responding to me. She was quiet, withdrawn, and did not pay much attention to me. I found this painful, but I also knew that she had a serious adjustment to make. I did not want to push her into accepting me with open arms. I wanted a genuine response from her, one that came from the heart. I would wait as long as it took. She appeared to be fine with our new living arrangement. I knew I could only wait and see how she would really feel once life took on a more stable routine.

Louie wanted me to feel right at home. I began to reorganize my surroundings in a way that I could better function in. But this process was slow and careful. I did not want to step on anyone's toes, but I also did not want to feel like a boarder in someone else's house. Louie would be my husband one day, and this would be our home. I needed to feel like I belonged.

As life in our new household took on a more relaxed pace, my back began to trouble me horribly. Tests and X-rays confirmed a serious problem, one that might mean more grief for my new family. I did not sleep as I replayed the doctor's voice in my head, and knew what I had to do. If it was as bad as the doctor suspected it to be, then I would end my relationship with Louie. He had lost Debbie only a short time ago. I did not want him to suffer any more loss because of me.

I was very afraid of what the morning would bring. I had told Louie my feelings, and he insisted that we would see through whatever it was together. Jennifer agreed. They would not walk away. It was the first time I really felt a sense of connection with another person. My fears of abandonment vanished. Instead of running away from trouble, my new family chose to face it head on with me. The meaning was clear: Louie was sending out his message of love and devotion to me.

I went into the hospital fearful that I would be told there was a tumor in my back. If I had an inoperable condition, I worried over what that would do to Louie and Jennifer. The MRI was a long, excruciating process that sapped my energy and left me even more afraid than before. I felt Louie with me the entire time, but inside I was praying hard. I asked God to see me through this, to help Louie and Jennifer if the news was bad.

After the MRI ended and I was led to the emergency room to await the results, the doctor returned with a concerned expression. It was a herniated and ruptured disc, and not a tumor. His explanation was drowned out by my inward joy at his news. The situation was operable, and I would be okay. This also meant that Louie and Jennifer would be spared the burden of grief because of me. I was happy and grateful. I needed surgery, but I had not fared well emotionally the last time I had gone under the knife. This time, however,

I had a family to support me.

I stayed in bed for a week in agonizing pain. The day of my surgery came as a welcome relief. Medication was only somewhat successful. I was glad when they wheeled me into the operating room. Though the work on my back was extensive, I awoke in my room some time later with no pain. I felt free and wonderful. It was the first time in years that I did not feel the dull ache in my back that had been a constant companion. I felt so healthy and relieved that I went home early, despite the surgery. I exercised and stretched my muscles, but inside I felt terrific. In three months I would marry the man I loved, and we would endure whatever was to come together. I was confident of Louie's feelings for me, and I was more than ready for what the next chapter of my life would bring.

My acceptance into the family was an important step towards my spiritual healing. I had undergone an enormous shift in my daily life, from Sister to everyday citizen. I thought I had a grasp on what that would mean for me, but there was a lot I needed to learn. My initial plans for moving away had changed radically when Louie came into my life. I had a family of my own now, and with that came responsibility and work. I was not a stand-in for Debbie, nor was I a ready-made mother. I did not know how my presence would be felt, and I did not know if it would be wanted.

The early days of our new arrangement were not always easy to bear, but they did renew my strength of purpose. There were times when I could not reach Jennifer, or some situation would prove to be more complicated than I had originally imagined, and I would ask myself if I could do this. Was I strong enough to keep going? Could I be a wife and mother? I thought my life would always be the church, but it had not turned out the way I had imagined. Could I succeed in this new role? Would I be able to offer the love and concern this family needs to thrive? Can I thrive here?

These questions followed me as I made Louie's home my home, and as I tried to cultivate a healthy relationship with Jennifer. There were days when I wanted to give up, and others where I would smile. I realized that I needed to take each day God gave me and work with it, carefully nurturing it so it would grow and create the seed for tomorrow. I was not out to win a mother or wife of the year award, but I did want to try my best. Some of that earlier perfectionism snuck through every once in a while, but I wanted us all to be happy in our new environment. And I knew that a lot of the burden fell on me.

Chapter 16

Louie and I were married on October 28th. It was a beautiful, moving, and touching ceremony. I had planned most of it with the same attention to detail I had given to my prayer services. Jennifer helped me select the bridesmaids' dresses, while Louie remained supportive and helped in any way he could.

It was not easy going from my Sister Linda mentality to a wedding gown. I selected the first one I fell in love with. I knew in my heart it was perfect for me. Each aspect of the wedding was planned with care and love. I wanted everyone to share in the day with us, and I also wanted to express the love Louie and I felt for each other in every gesture, reading, and song that we selected for our new life together.

The vows I took on that wonderful day were far different from the ones I had recited over 25 years before. Then, I had been an unsure girl with a hope for a bright future filled with promise. I was older now, and had lived through much since those promises were made. This time, however, every word I spoke came directly from the deepest place in my heart, and not an ounce of doubt clouded our wedding day. I knew I had at last found my purpose, that strange feeling that had eluded me for so long, and that I could never quite grasp. As I looked into Louie's eyes and recognized all the love he had for me in his happy, smiling face, I knew I had at last found my answer. That odd feeling of uncertainty would not bother me again.

At the end of the ceremony, we released two pure, white doves as a symbol of our new life together. I had finally found freedom in my love for Louie, and in facing my fears of the past and the unknown future. Louie had also dealt with his own pain and grief, and the doves were visible proof that we were ready to move forward with each other.

The love that surrounded the day was palpable. I had never felt so close to my family. We were gathered together for a happy, joyous occasion. I had so often seen them all on such sad, painful days. It was a blessing and a miracle to share in nothing, but good news with them. I also found a special connection with Jennifer. Through tears the three of us danced together as the reception wound down. I felt her love enter me as we stood there united as a family. For me, it was the final confirmation that this was indeed the purpose God had planned for me.

As the years have passed, I have come to an understanding of myself, and this is something that I would never have been able to grasp if the events in my life had not unfolded the way they did. God's plan for me was waiting all along. I just needed to recognize it. I had blamed myself for years over insecurities, fears, and disappointments. I had questioned my life extensively and not reached a solution. I had also wondered if I was lovable enough, and wanted enough, to be accepted by anyone in this world.

As time passed and our family became more centered, Jennifer grew older and found a love of her own. As she prepared for her new life, much like I once had only a few short years before, she turned to those present and said, "I'd like you to meet my mom and dad." As tears filled my eyes, I understood at long last that yes, I have always been loved and wanted. And I had finally learned to forgive myself for that, too.

Throughout my story, I have shared what it means to forgive ourselves for the choices we make in life, for the insecurities we often feel as we stumble along in uncertainty, and for the fears we hide behind because they are our safety net and crutch. Today, I challenge you to take a good, long look at where your life has led you, and where you would next like it to go. Ask yourself if you have made the most of the gifts you have been given, and if you have lived up to the purpose God has set aside for you. If not, begin today. Push past the hindrances in your path and promise yourself a better tomorrow. I did it, and I have faith that you can too.

Part Six-A Final Thought

This short story was borrowed from my parish bulletin. I think it's a wonderful reminder of what it means to allow forgiveness into our lives. It has provided me with much insight, and I hope it will for you too.

A Tale of Two Friends

Two friends were walking through the desert. As they were walking along they had an argument, and one friend slapped the other one in the face. The one who got slapped was hurt, but without saying anything, he wrote in the sand:
"Today my best friend slapped me in the face."
They kept on walking until they found an oasis with a large pool of water in the center of it and they decided to take a bath. The one who had been slapped got stuck in the mud and started to drown, but his friend saved him. After he recovered from the near drowning, he carved on a stone:
"Today my best friend saved my life."
The friend who had slapped and then saved his best friend asked him, "After I hurt you, you wrote in the sand, but now you carve on a stone. Why?"
The other friend replied, "When someone hurts us, we should write it down in sand where the winds of forgiveness can erase it away, but when someone does something good for us, we must engrave it in stone where no wind can ever erase it."

Learn to write your hurts in the sand and to carve your blessings in stone!

Printed in the United States
17100LVS00005B/304-1074